"This is a book about the infir................................. of holiness and love, who wants to .... erately need: Himself. T. W. Hunt is a master of the spiritual life and leads us to a deep appropriation of the gift of transforming faith. This is a book for everyone who loves Jesus and wants to know Him better."

—TIMOTHY GEORGE, chairman, America's
National Prayer Committee

"The writings of T. W. Hunt have been used of God for many years to strengthen and encourage believers toward a greater love for Him and a deeper piety. This most recent work, *Seeing the Unseen*, is certainly no exception. In fact, it addresses matters of faith and spiritual formation with pastoral sensitivity and conviction of our loving Trinitarian God. Important theological truths are communicated clearly and accessibly for a wide readership. I trust that this marvelously helpful volume will be used of God in days to come to influence and shape a generation of Christ followers in their walk with God so that they will be better equipped to make a difference for the cause of Christ and His kingdom."

—DR. DAVID DOCKERY, president, Union University,
Jackson, Tennessee

"The reader of *Seeing the Unseen* has the rare privilege of climbing the mountain of truth with a trusted guide, Dr. T. W. Hunt. He is the greatest embodiment of Christlike nobility I have ever known. His years of intimacy with Jesus help us seek God and see His invisible ways and works. So many are like Israel, seeing the acts of God but not knowing His ways, as Moses did. T. W. Hunt has been a spiritual mentor and father to me for almost thirty-five years. He will guide you into the rarefied air of true faith that he has been believing for years. The view is worth the climb. Sit at his feet; follow in his steps. You will want to read this book again and again."

—HAYES WICKER, pastor, First Baptist Church, Naples, Florida

SEEING *THE* UNSEEN

Cultivate a Faith That Unveils the Hidden Presence *of* God

T. W. HUNT

NAVPRESS ◐

Discipleship Inside Out™

NavPress is the publishing ministry of The Navigators, an international Christian organization and leader in personal spiritual development. NavPress is committed to helping people grow spiritually and enjoy lives of meaning and hope through personal and group resources that are biblically rooted, culturally relevant, and highly practical.

For a free catalog go to www.NavPress.com
or call 1.800.366.7788 in the United States or 1.800.839.4769 in Canada.

ISBN-13: 978-1-61521-581-2

Cover design by Gearbox
Cover image by Masterfile

Some of the anecdotal illustrations in this book are true to life and are included with the permission of the persons involved. All other illustrations are composites of real situations, and any resemblance to people living or dead is coincidental.

Unless otherwise identified, all Scripture quotations in this publication are taken from the Holman Christian Standard Bible (HCSB). Copyright © 1999, 2000, 2002, 2003 by Holman Bible Publishers, Nashville Tennessee. All rights reserved. Other versions used include: The Holy Bible, English Standard Version (ESV), copyright © 2001 by Crossway Bibles, a division of Good News Publishers. Used by permission. All rights reserved; the New King James Version (NKJV). Copyright © 1982 by Thomas Nelson, Inc. Used by permission. All rights reserved; the *Holy Bible*, New Living Translation (NLT), copyright © 1996, 2004. Used by permission of Tyndale House Publishers, Inc., Wheaton, Illinois 60189. All rights reserved; the *Holy Bible, New International Version*® (NIV®). Copyright © 1973, 1978, 1984 by International Bible Society. Used by permission of Zondervan. All rights reserved; the New American Standard Bible® (NASB), Copyright © 1960, 1962, 1963, 1968, 1971, 1972, 1973, 1975, 1977, 1995 by The Lockman Foundation. Used by permission; the *Revised Standard Version Bible* (RSV), copyright 1946, 1952, 1971, by the Division of Christian Education of the National Council of the Churches of Christ in the USA, used by permission, all rights reserved; *THE MESSAGE* (MSG). Copyright © 1993, 1994, 1995, 1996, 2000, 2001, 2002. Used by permission of NavPress Publishing Group; the *Good News Bible Today's English Version* (TEV), copyright © American Bible Society 1966, 1971, 1976, 1992; the *Amplified Bible* (AMP), © The Lockman Foundation 1954, 1958, 1962, 1964, 1965, 1987; the New Century Version (NCV). Copyright © 1987, 1988, 1991 by Thomas Nelson, Inc. Used by permission. All rights reserved; the *Modern Language Bible: The Berkeley Version in Modern English* (MLB), copyright © 1945, 1959, 1969 by Zondervan Publishing House, used by permission; *the New Testament: An Expanded Translation* by Kenneth S. Wuest, © Wm. B. Eerdmans Publishing Co. 1961. Used by permission; The Jerusalem Bible (JB), 1966, 1967 and 1968 by Darton, Longman & Todd Ltd and Doubleday and Co. Inc.; the King James Version (KJV); the American Standard Version (ASV); Darby Translation (DARBY), Young's Literal Translation (YLT); The Latin Vulgate; the Martin Bible; and Reina-Valera 1995 (RVR 1995). Copyright © 1995 by United Bible Societies.

Library of Congress Cataloging-in-Publication Data
Hunt, T. W., 1929-
  Seeing the unseen : cultivate a faith that unveils the hidden presence of God / T. W. Hunt.
       p. cm.
  Includes bibliographical references.
  ISBN 978-1-61521-581-2
  1. Hidden God. 2. Faith. I. Title.
  BT180.H54H86 2011
  234'.23--dc22
                           2011000236

Printed in the United States of America

1 2 3 4 5 6 7 8 / 16 15 14 13 12 11

Soli Deo Gloria

CONTENTS

INTRODUCTION

I was raised in a devout Christian home that had daily devotions. While growing up, I was not taught I had to see the unseen. The unseen was such an integral part of our family life that it never occurred to me to question that God was hearing our prayers. Indeed, at times I experienced such a sense of reality that I knew God was in the room, registering our prayers.

I was far into my adult life before I realized that for many people prayer is unreal. My colleagues often doubted God's existence. At times the prayers I heard in church struck me as humdrum and routine rather than alive and vibrant. Other times, however, I heard a magnificent saint pray in such a way that I knew he or she was connecting with God.

These differences struck a chord in my spirit, and I began to search for the meaning of "seeing the unseen" (see 2 Corinthians 4:18). This book is a product of that searching. I pray it will answer questions many Christians are afraid to verbalize.

The chapters are short. I felt a need to summarize the main thrust of the book in the last chapter. I did not want to offend the reader with needless repetition but felt strongly that he or she needed the reaffirmation I had tried to stress.

I have avoided references to the spectacular visions

occasionally given to a child of God, such as Elisha's seeing the chariots of God on the mountainside and praying that his servant would also see them (see 2 Kings 6:17) or Peter's vision of the angel sent to free him from prison (see Acts 12:7-10). I want this book to help the average person, who is not likely to have such impressive visions. If an Elisha or a Peter reads this book, God will lead that person to a relationship that will allow more magnificent visions. I hope the average reader will not be disappointed if he or she fails to see spectacular signs. God is constantly speaking to all of His children, and we all need to be aware of the supernatural, which is always present, whether we are at our desk, in the kitchen, or driving down the road.

Our world is in ever-increasing crises of belief and morality. If ever God's people need to tap into the unseen by real faith, that time is now. May God open your eyes to the vast realm of reality that is usually unperceived by His people. My prayers are with the readers of this book.

CHAPTER ONE

A STRANGE COMMAND

We do not focus on what is seen, but on what is unseen;
for what is seen is temporary, but what is unseen is eternal.

2 CORINTHIANS 4:18

VARYING PHILOSOPHIES

The world today overflows with conflicting philosophies. Each philosophy—atheism, agnosticism, humanism, pantheism, panentheism, false religions, animism, and a wide variety of cults—clamors for the attention of the world's inhabitants. Yet in the western world, the philosophy of materialism unconsciously dominates the minds of most people.

Materialism is not consciously taught in schools or churches; our ambience and the overarching worldviews of our relatives and friends infuse it into us. Early in our lives we are taught that position, power, fame, wealth, and all their accoutrements are the main goals we should seek.

Even followers of Christ are somewhat divided, not only

between theism and deism but also by doctrines or varieties of entertainment. Christians are seeking position, power, fame, or wealth *within the church.*

To see the unseen, we must begin with the currently "seen." Please hang in there with me. I'll be using some scientific terms, but they are important to our understanding of the unseen. We'll start with the two laws of thermodynamics, which you have likely encountered before.

LAWS OF THE PHYSICAL WORLD

Physicists tell us that two immutable laws govern all creation. The first law — the conservation of energy — is that all energy is preserved and cannot be destroyed. It can change forms, and thereby much useful energy is lost. For example, a car engine sends its waste energy into an exhaust pipe and then out into the atmosphere.

Entropy, the second law, tells us that all systems are winding down. All systems tend to move from order to disorder. We see this in the deterioration of our bodies as they age; various parts of the body gradually become more and more useless. Astronomers tell us that the galaxies in the universe are expanding by means of a dark or unknown energy. As this happens, the fuel in the centers of stars is being exhausted (although new stars are also being formed). Ultimately, the expansion and exhaustion of fuel will lead to a cold death in the universe. We Christians know, of course, that God can interrupt the tendency toward a disordered universe for His own wise and magnificent purposes. Yet, at present, no system or process in the universe can halt the progress of disorder, or entropy.

However, these two laws apply to only the physical world. What of the spiritual world?

THE SPIRITUAL WORLD

Although things in the physical world tend toward decay and entropy, that is not the case in the spiritual world. In the spiritual world, things move toward perfection. God's purpose for Christians is that we grow upward and forward in sanctification. He wants us to move from babyhood to adulthood so that we might become completed persons, ready for a never-ending fellowship with Christ.

A term from philosophy first introduced by Aristotle, *entelechy*, can help us better understand this spiritual tendency to Christlike perfection brought about by the Holy Spirit. Aristotle used this term for the full realization of form out of process. For example, the entelechy of an acorn is to be an oak tree, the entelechy of a caterpillar is to be a butterfly, the entelechy of a new believer is to be a mature disciple of Christ, and so on. Entelechy makes actual what is otherwise merely potential. Later philosophers used the term to refer to the life-giving force that moves us to self-fulfillment.

All of the upward movement or growth is fulfilled in the spiritual realm, the unseen reality, which we cannot perceive with our physical eyes. However, God at times provides us with evidence of an unseen force—for example, the occurrence of miracles and the complex design of the universe.

SEE THE UNSEEN

In addition, the Bible repeatedly assures us that we can "see" this unseen world.

Through all the centuries probably no other verse in Scripture has been more misunderstood or misdirected than Paul's instruction to the Corinthian church, "So we do not focus on what is seen, but on what is unseen" (2 Corinthians 4:18). The only "real" world has always been what we can see or hear with our physical body. As widespread as the Christian church is, even within the body we concentrate on visible results rather than on the invisible. In our everyday lives, we constantly shift our attention from the current conversation, or the potatoes, or the desk work, or the road on which we are driving. We concentrate on the visible rather than on the spiritual growth available to us if we can learn to look at the invisible.

Because of our material upbringing, it doesn't make sense to "look at" that which is invisible. That's why to focus on it requires a different kind of attention. To focus on the unseen requires being aware that the unseen is the always-present background of something other than what we can touch or manipulate. It means considering the unseen in every decision and act. It means not focusing on entropy but on entelechy. Physically we are moving toward death, but spiritually we, even now, are participating in eternal factors that have a wondrous end.

EVIDENCE FOR THE UNSEEN

People today acknowledge that there are factors in this world that are not visible to the naked eye. For instance, most of us have never seen an electron or a black hole, but we believe that they exist, on the authority of scientists who have empirically authenticated their existence. These scientists speak from a proof that either derives from various kinds of equipment or from mathematical or theoretical deductions that were provable.

Similarly, the centuries since Christ have produced many great saints who believed in a spiritual world that we cannot see with our eyes or hear with our ears. The huge extent of their numbers and the quality of their lives demonstrate that they somehow really saw something beyond the physical world. Many believed so strongly in the unseen spiritual world that they were willing to die for the cause of Christ. It is easier for us in the Christian world to accept their word because their conclusions often changed the world. These "authorities" are believable.

Genuinely spiritual people often seem to this world to act foolishly because "the natural man does not welcome what comes from God's Spirit, because it is foolishness to him; he is not able to know it since it is evaluated spiritually" (1 Corinthians 2:14). Because the natural world is most obvious to our physical senses, even devout believers often unconsciously rely on the materially perceptible rather than looking beyond for spiritual messages or meanings.

The same was true in Jesus' time. Many did not believe His words, so He warned, "Anyone who has ears should listen!" (Matthew 13:9). After the parable of the sower, Jesus told His disciples, "Your eyes are blessed because they do see, and your ears because they do hear! For I assure you: Many prophets and righteous people longed to see the things you see yet didn't see them; to hear the things you hear yet didn't hear them" (verses 16-17). In some way, the disciples had ears and eyes that most people did not have.

THE PERMANENCE OF THE SPIRITUAL

When we realize that many worldly pleasures are ephemeral and deceptive, we place more importance on spiritual vision. The nature of truly spiritual pleasures has an enduring quality that makes temporary pleasures, such as overeating or wrongful sex, worth doing without. Paul's mind was fixed on the permanence of the eternal: "Hope that is seen is not hope, because who hopes for what he sees? But if we hope for what we do not see, we eagerly wait for it with patience" (Romans 8:24-25). Blessedly, God has ordained many worthwhile perceptible pleasures, but John cautions us that

> *Everything that belongs to the world — the lust of the flesh, the lust of the eyes, and the pride in one's lifestyle — is not from the Father, but is from the world. And the world with its lust is passing away, but the one who does God's will remains forever.* (1 JOHN 2:15-17)

SEEING AND HEARING

Spiritual darkness within is blindness. Jesus preached, "The eye is the lamp of the body. If your eye is good, your whole body will be full of light. But if your eye is bad, your whole body will be full of darkness. So if the light within you is darkness — how deep is that darkness" (Matthew 6:22-23). Yet at times, even the most sensitive of us experience periods of darkness. Righteous Job cried out, "If He passes by me, I wouldn't see Him; if He goes right by, I wouldn't recognize Him" (Job 9:11). But proper seeing is essential to obedience. Isaiah quotes the Lord:

> *Listen, you deaf!*
> *Look, you blind, so that you may see.*

Who is blind but My servant,

or deaf like My messenger I am sending?

Who is blind like My dedicated one,

or blind like the servant of the LORD*?*

Though seeing many things, *you do not obey.*

Though his ears are open, he does not listen. (42:18-20, EMPHASIS ADDED)

Paul ordered New Testament slaves to be obedient: "Don't work only while being watched, in order to please men" (Ephesians 6:6).

It is also true that blindness and deafness to God can be deliberate. This was the case with Stephen's executioners. They "stopped their ears" (Acts 7:57). Jesus said, on the other hand, that the perceptivity of the disciples was blessed. The Jewish leaders made their choice; the disciples also made a choice. We believe what we want to believe.

The plethora of competing philosophies and disagreements among theologians is confusing to readers whose minds are open. As they plow their way through such conflicting ideas, they occasionally find something that strikes a spark — "This is right!" Truth, ultimately, is known by revelation. While that may seem arbitrary, it was not arbitrary to the fishermen and the assorted lot who believed Jesus when He spoke.

Our outlook may be a product of many unconscious factors: parents, authorities, environment, personal tastes, desires, and/ or many other unsuspected components. In my own case, when I stumble onto some truth that I know to be valid, I check the truth against Scripture and against the person and personality of Jesus.

Part of Jesus' commissioning speech (a partial quotation of Isaiah 61:1-3) claimed that the Spirit of the Lord had anointed

Him to give recovery of sight to the blind (see Luke 4:18). Proper perception of the unseen is an act of God. When Jesus denounced the Pharisees' blindness, He said that if they should turn He would "cure them" (Matthew 13:15). Our understanding depends not on ourselves but on the Spirit of God's leading us.

Spiritual sight was also important in the Old Testament. It seems likely that Jesus' parable of Lazarus and the rich man derived from His familiarity with the psalmist's plaint in Psalm 17:13-15, where the writer contrasts those whose "portion is in this life" with his own awareness that he would be satisfied with the likeness of the Lord when he awoke.

FACTORS IN SEEING

If Jesus had revealed His Messiahship and kingship openly, He would have had a huge following looking for the wrong purposes. He often obscured kingdom principles by the use of parables. Although the disciples perceived the spiritual principles in His teaching slowly, in process, over a long period of time, Jesus contrasted their seeing and hearing with that of the religious authorities in hard-hitting terms. He told His followers,

Isaiah's prophecy [6:9-10] is fulfilled in them, which says:

You will listen and listen,
yet never understand;
and you will look and look,
yet never perceive.
For this people's heart has grown callous;
their ears are hard of hearing,

and they have shut their eyes;

otherwise they might see with their eyes

and hear with their ears,

understand with their hearts

and turn back—

and I would cure them. (MATTHEW 13:14-16)

This alarming threat moves us to consider what blinds and deafens us to the real world of the spiritual.

SPIRITUAL BLINDERS

Paul called that blinder "the flesh." He cautioned the church in Rome that "the mind-set of the flesh is hostile to God because it does not submit itself to God's law, for it is unable to do so" (Romans 8:7). He assured the church that they were not "in the flesh, but in the Spirit, since the Spirit of God lives in you" (verse 9). In Christ, we are a new creation (see Galatians 6:15).

I believe the most significant blinder for most of us is mind wandering. Long ago I discovered that if I ask the Holy Spirit to convey to me a sense of reality while I pray, I am overwhelmed with consciousness of the prayer I am praying. I become almost oblivious to my surroundings and have a strong sense of the overwhelming presence of God with me.

Notice that Genesis 5:24 does not say that God walked with Enoch but that Enoch walked with God. *God is always with us.* Noah walked with God (see Genesis 6:9). What's missing for most of us is our consciousness that God is with us. We fail to drink in God's presence. Ephesians 6:18 admonishes us to be alert in prayer. Through the Spirit, we can develop an awareness of the presence of God, a sense of the reality of His holy presence.

Jesus cautioned, "Whatever is born of the flesh is flesh, and whatever is born of the Spirit is spirit" (John 3:6). His teaching showed that the problem is not that God has not revealed Himself to us but that "the flesh" and "the world" blind us and prevent us from looking beyond the immediate.

In the parable of the sower, Jesus warned us about the pervasiveness of flesh in the world. In the parable of the seeds, He pointed out that the seed sown among thorns "is one who hears the word, but the worries of this age and the seduction of wealth choke the word, and it becomes unfruitful" (Matthew 13:22). The parable of the rich young ruler who chose wealth over following Jesus (see 19:16-22) amply illustrates this truth.

Paul urged the Colossian church to live in the reality of the unseen:

> Seek what is above. . . . Set your minds on what is above, not on what is on the earth. For you have died, and your life is hidden with the Messiah in God. When the Messiah, who is your life, is revealed, then you will also be revealed with Him in glory. (COLOSSIANS 3:1-4)

People have had difficulty seeing the unseen since the days of Noah. It becomes especially challenging in times of trouble. In preparing the Corinthian church for their persecution and to encourage these believers to endure, Paul wrote,

> We do not give up; even though our outer person is being destroyed [chapters 4 and 6 of 2 Corinthians briefly name Paul's sufferings], our inner person is being renewed day by day. For our momentary light affliction is producing for us an absolutely incomparable eternal weight of glory. (2 CORINTHIANS 4:16-17)

To endure, we must focus on the unseen.

CHAPTER TWO

THE ROLE OF FAITH

Anyone who has ears should listen!
MATTHEW 13:9

BEYOND THE PHYSICAL

God encourages us to look beyond what is physically apparent
to the spiritual forces behind the physical ones. A spiritual God
created a physical universe. Moses told the Israelites, "Only be
on your guard and diligently watch yourselves, so that you don't
forget the things your eyes have seen and so that they don't slip
from your mind" (Deuteronomy 4:9). Throughout Scripture the
word *mind* usually refers not to the physiological brain but to
the *inner* (spiritual) thinking process. We might say the mind is
the cognitive organ of the spirit.[1]

At times the words *mind* and *heart* seem interchangeable. In
this passage, Moses cautioned the children of Israel that the
physical miracles they had seen, such as the ten plagues and the
crossing of the Red Sea, were backed by spiritual forces more

important than their visible results. Later, Proverbs 4:23 enjoined the Israelites, "Guard your *heart* above all else, for it is the source of life" (emphasis added). The prophets too made repeated efforts to redirect the nation from legalistic religious observance to inner worship.

Jesus' words to Thomas, who doubted the Resurrection and demanded physical proof of it, underscore that the spiritual reality overshadows physical reality. In reproaching Thomas, Jesus laid down the principle "Because you have seen Me, you have believed. Those who believe without seeing are blessed" (John 20:29). Proper, genuine believing without seeing physical proof gives a special blessing.

However, God's grace often allows the physical to prove the spiritual. Jesus showed Thomas the proof that he demanded, and Thomas's faith grew. All of the disciples had to have physical proof of the Resurrection. However, Jesus' spiritual force always preceded His physical actions.

TO BELIEVE OR NOT TO BELIEVE

Ultimately, belief is a matter of choice. Repeated warnings for us to make godly choices permeate the New Testament. When discussing which day of the week various early Christians set aside for worship, Paul referred the question back to a believer's individual faith: "Each one must be fully convinced in his own mind" (Romans 14:5). Faith *is* conviction. John wrote that truly loving others in word and deed would convince nonbelievers that believers knew the way of truth; their actions would be a demonstration of genuine faith (see 1 John 3).

Paul's words to the Romans reiterate that belief is a choice: "To set the mind on the flesh is death, but to set the mind on the Spirit is life and peace" (Romans 8:6, ESV). Peter urged the Colossians to "be clear-headed and disciplined for prayer" (1 Peter 4:7). While all initiative is, ultimately, with God, He assigns us various roles in working out the specific details of His work. We are fully convinced in our faith, meaning no doubt enters the fact of our faith. Even so, God sometimes supplies physical proof for the sake of our faith.

EXPECTED TO HAVE FAITH

God *expects* us to have faith; it is the mechanism by which we see the unseen.

When the disciples were frightened in the storm, Jesus asked them, "Why are you fearful? Do you still have no faith?" (Mark 4:40) — that is, "Do you not see the source of My works?" They had witnessed Jesus repeatedly exercising His powers and physically demonstrating the unseen. He was exhorting His followers to see the unseen through the eyes of faith, to see God at work. He had given them lots of physical proof of His powers; they only had to choose to believe He was still at work in the unseen. This ability to see what most people miss fulfills the longing of the ages. Jesus told His disciples, "Many prophets and righteous people longed to see the things you see yet didn't see them; to hear the things you hear yet didn't hear them" (Matthew 13:17).

Paul wrote, "Everything that is not from faith is sin" (Romans 14:23). Faith, the ability to see the unseen, should permeate *all* our actions and thinking. Faith inherits the biblical promises: "We want each of you to demonstrate the same diligence for the final realization of your hope, so that you won't become lazy, but imitators of those who inherit the promises through faith and perseverance" (Hebrews 6:11-12). The writer of Hebrews assures us that "without faith it is impossible to please God, for the one who draws near to Him must believe that He exists and rewards those who seek Him" (11:6).

EXPECTED TO HEAR THE INAUDIBLE

Scripture also admonishes us to hear the inaudible. Eight times in the New Testament, we are informed that anyone who has ears should listen (see Matthew 11:15; 13:9; Mark 4:9,23; Luke 8:8; 14:35; Revelation 2:11; 13:9). God expects us to listen for the inaudible. When the disciples' faith failed because they had no bread, Jesus asked them, "Don't you understand yet?" (Mark 8:21).

If God tells us to listen for His voice, He intends to speak to us. One of the earliest factors in learning faith is realizing that all the biblical evidence indicates that God will indeed be communicating with us. Also important is *how* we listen. With that injunction, Jesus attaches a promise: "Take care *how* you listen. For whoever has, more will be given to him; and whoever does not have, even what he thinks he has will be taken away" (Luke 8:18, emphasis added). Moses grasped this principle. Having found favor with God, he asked Him for more: "If I have indeed found favor in Your sight, please teach me Your ways, and I will know You and find favor in Your sight" (Exodus 33:13). The more we receive from God, the more God gives us. The opposite is also true: The more we ignore His words to us, the more He removes His word from us.

THE OUTER AND THE INNER

Faith comes from seeing and hearing with spiritual eyes. Jesus commanded us to "stop judging according to outward appearances; rather judge according to righteous judgment" (John 7:24). This prohibition would not have been necessary if people were looking at other people through spiritual eyes. Most of us "judge according to outward appearances"—that is, with our physical eyes instead of our spirit's "vision." Note that Jesus contrasted outward judgment with righteous judgment, not with inner judgment. As He emphasized in the Sermon on the Mount, true righteousness can spring only from the indwelling Christ; it can never be a matter of performance.

While experience teaches us that most people choose according to the physical (according to appetite) rather than the spiritual, Hebrews 5:14 establishes that spiritual eyes can be developed: "Solid food is for the mature—for those whose [spiritual] senses have been trained to distinguish between good and evil." Here is evidence of entelechy in the spiritual realm. A believer's training is one of the factors sanctifying us, moving us upward and forward toward Christlike perfection.

Physical pleasures are nearly always fleeting; we forget the satisfaction as soon as it is gratified. However, if we can learn to hear His voice, the ever-present Spirit of God imparts an enduring quality to spiritual pleasures. The presence of the Spirit is in itself a joy that never ends.

Most of God's people want to have faith. When the father of the demon-possessed boy asked Jesus to heal his son if He could, Jesus corrected him, saying "'If You can?' Everything is possible to the one who believes" (Mark 9:23). The father immediately appealed to Jesus, "I do believe! Help my unbelief" (verse 24). Most of us identify easily with the father's words. We too desire to believe, to have faith in the unseen. The disciples certainly did. Having often seen Jesus pray, they pled with Him to teach them to pray as John the Baptist taught his disciples (see Luke

11:1). On another occasion they asked Him to increase their faith (see 17:5).

WHAT PROPER SEEING ACCOMPLISHES

Jesus' reply indicates the magnitude of what prayer can accomplish. He told them, "If you have faith the size of a mustard seed . . . you can say to this mulberry tree, 'Be uprooted and planted in the sea,' and it will obey you" (Luke 17:6). This is one of many indications about the magnificence that faith in His promises can accomplish.

For example, in Matthew 7:9-10, in His instruction on prayer, Jesus points out that a father would not give dangerous gifts when a child was asking for bread or fish, and then says, "If you then, who are evil, know how to give good gifts to your children, how much more will your Father in heaven give good gifts to those who ask Him!" (verse 11).

In Luke 11, He gives the example of a man who goes to a friend at midnight and asks for bread. The request is initially denied but was then granted due to the man's persistence. Perseverance is a quality of faith.

In Luke 18:1-8, we again see what persistence in faith can accomplish, when the persistent widow obtains justice from the judge.

Faith plays a vital role in seeing the unseen; it is a choice to believe that the size of our request is no problem for omnipotence.

CHAPTER THREE

WHAT FAITH IS

Faith is the reality of what is hoped for,
the proof of what is not seen.

HEBREWS 11:1

THE MEANING OF FAITH

Martin Luther's translation of the Bible gives a sense of the meaning of Hebrews 11:1: *Es ist aber der Glaube eine gewisse Zuversicht des, das man hofft, and nicht zweifeln an des, und ein Nichtzweifeln an dem, das man nicht sieht*: "It is, however, the belief, a definite confidence in what one hopes for, and does not doubt on the basis of what one does not see." Faith is an unshakeable confidence, given by the Holy Spirit, that God will actually do what He says and that He will do what we ask.

The following various translations of the word for "reality" in Hebrews 11:1 (*hupóstasis*) show us the difficulty in determining its exact meaning:

- "assurance" (ESV, NASB, ASV, RSV)
- "substance" (KJV, NKJV)
- "reality" (HCSB)
- "the confirmation, the title deed" (AMP)
- "title deed" (Wuest)
- "being sure" (NIV, NCV)
- "substantiating" (DARBY)
- "confidence" (NLT, YLT)
- "to be sure" (TEV)
- "solid ground" (MLB)
- "trust in God" (MSG)
- "only faith can guarantee" (JB)
- "*fides sperandarum*," or "expectant faith" (Vulgate, Latin)
- "*la foi rend présentes les choses qu'on espère*," or "faith renders present the things one hopes for" (Martin, French)
- "certeza," or "certainty" (RVR 1995, Spanish)

The overarching theme running through all of these translations is the sense of reality. If we are gripped by a sense of reality, doubt will not be possible. We will not be swayed by outward circumstances. While it's true that God, who is omnipresent, hears all prayers, skillful and unpracticed, when that sense of reality grips me, I have a strong inner conviction that I am in direct address to God. I *know* real dialogue between myself and the Creator's purpose for me for that day.

Obviously, the god of this world, the father of lies, will do all in his power to obscure reality from us. Jesus emphasized this in the parable of the sower. Second Corinthians 4:4 tells us flatly that "the god of this age has blinded the minds of unbelievers."

The emphasis of the entire New Testament, from Matthew through Revelation, is on the certainty of what we cannot see.

THE ROLE OF THE HOLY SPIRIT AND LOOKING TO JESUS

Certainty is faith, which is a fruit of God's Spirit (see Galatians 5:22). Some are given a special gift of faith (see 1 Corinthians 12:9). The Spirit reveals the deep things of God (see 1 Corinthians 2:10). Jesus promised that the Holy Spirit would teach the disciples "all things" (John 14:26). After emphasizing that the present world could not reveal the things of God, Paul informs the Corinthians, "We also speak these things, not in words taught by human wisdom, but in those taught by the Spirit, explaining spiritual things to spiritual people" (1 Corinthians 2:13).

The Spirit's work is to magnify Christ (see John 16:14). Jesus' life is an example of entelechy, resulting in the goal of the various factors and decisions of His life. Paul tells us that we are to be "rooted and built up in [Christ] and established in the faith" (Colossians 2:7). In order to be established, we must be "rooted and built up" in the Lord Jesus. He, through the Spirit, is the source of our faith. "Faith comes from what is heard, and what is heard comes through the message about Christ" (Romans 10:17).

The Spirit will help us learn of Christ through the New Testament and His ever-present work in us. Following the Spirit's leading, we will learn the life and works of the Son of God. The work of the Spirit—Him imparting the awareness of Christ in us—is the secret to building biblical faith. The more we know Jesus through the Spirit, the greater our faith will be.

We will grow to be more and more like Him; our entelechy will more and more match His.

About a year ago, I was again studying the life of Christ and became acutely aware that Jesus was always conscious of His Father in that He was constantly in prayer. When Jesus was healing, He was praying; when He was teaching, He was praying; when He was eating, He was praying. Because 1 Thessalonians 5:17 tells us to pray constantly, I wondered if such a life would be possible to me, so I asked the Lord to make my prayer life 24/7.

A NEW OUTLOOK on LIFE

The effect of this was almost more than I had asked for. I became more appreciative and noticed that I was thankful for little details I had scarcely noticed before. I was on the lookout for God's purposes in all my conversation. God established ("rooted and built up") the supremacy of Christ in every detail and aspect of my life. God was implanting the factors of entelechy in my life. I was growing into my potential of being like Christ.

The "with you always" aspect of this new 24/7 orientation affected even my conversation. I started living in the reality that God hears what I say to everyone and began to phrase my daily conversations in such a way that it would also suit God's purposes.

To help you understand what I mean, let me put it another way. Let's say I'm talking with Bob and Jim. While I'm directing my words at Jim, I know that what I am saying to him will have an effect on Bob, so I don't say anything that would offend Bob; Bob's personality and life affect what I say to Jim. Similarly, I strive to live in such a way that who God is affects all that I do and say. This parallels the ever-present direction of the Spirit in our lives. He knows and hears everything we do and say. This has sometimes meant I had to deflect my attitude toward my wife to be that of Christ toward His bride, the church. At other times this kind of consciousness means I suddenly realize that the next bite will be sin. And occasionally it electrifies the singing and praise going on in a church service.

DIRECTING OUR CONSCIOUSNESS

My hope is that as you will begin to apply these two concepts: (1) praying consciously or unconsciously 24/7, and (2) living in the certainty that God is and will do what His Word says. I pray that this consciousness will so permeate your heart that you will pray for these two ideals to dominate your prayer life. I realize that many cult leaders have strong convictions about their errors, but two things can assure us that we are following the centuries-old orthodoxy of the central Christian faith: (1) we are sticking as strictly as possible to the biblical injunctions and examples, and (2) a sense of separateness, of holiness, will permeate our faithfulness and then be a permanent part of our thinking.

The many directives on faith in the New Testament reflect the various writers' consciousness of faith in the Old Testament. They had an unerring sense of the reality of God; so did the Old Testament saints. This explains why Abraham could leave Ur and why he believed God regardless of the seemingly impossible promise that his offspring would be as numerous as the stars (see Genesis 15:5).

The opposite of this is also true. Israel's lack of faith occurred in spite of the many miracles they had witnessed. Physical proof did not always exact biblical faith. Although the crowds had observed many of Jesus' miracles, after the famous Bread of Life sermon, they demanded even more than He had wisely given, and they deserted Him (see John 6:66).

After that mass desertion, Jesus challenged the disciples: "You don't want to go away too, do you?" (verse 67). Peter's answer shows that he was already rooted, built up, and established in the certainty that is faith: "Lord, who will we go to? You have the words of eternal *life*" (verse 68, emphasis added).

BIBLICAL EXAMPLES OF ASSURANCE

Biblical faith is the key to life (see John 3:16) and to righteousness (see Romans 4:22). Having life and righteousness, the disciple will act on faith. Look at Abraham, David, Isaiah, John, Peter, or Paul, for example. None of these men was perfect. They simply crossed the barrier set up by the world system. All who believe in the present certainty of God have access to whole new realms, opening up enormous possibilities, as exemplified in God's promises. These lend credence to the worldview that God "exists and rewards those who seek Him" (Hebrews 11:6).

The certainty of their faith helped these saints endure, sometimes through great difficulties. Abraham, whose wife, Sarah, was past the age of childbearing, believed God when He told him that he would be the father of many nations. Joshua believed God when He told him that his small band of men would win the battle against a huge, powerful army. "We have become companions of the Messiah if we hold firmly until the end the reality that we had at the start" (Hebrews 3:14). Faith enables endurance.

WHERE TO DIRECT OUR ATTENTION

This sense of reality talked about in Hebrews 11:1 is rooted in who God is, not in the particular request we are praying for. When Jehoshaphat was surrounded by three enemy armies, he prayed a prayer we need to practice: "We do not know what to do, but we look to You" (2 Chronicles 20:12). He was not telling God to rout the antagonistic forces; instead, he told God that he looked only to Him. Similarly, the psalmist did not describe his predicament; he prayed, "My eyes are always on the LORD, for He will pull my feet out of the net" (Psalm 25:15). The psalmist also looked only to God:

> Like a servant's eyes on His master's hand,
> like a servant girl's eyes on her mistress's hand,
> so our eyes are on the LORD our God
> until He shows us favor. (PSALM 123:2)

That great epitome of faith, Abraham, obeyed God, not on the basis of what he knew but rather on the basis of the wisdom of the Lord: "By faith Abraham, when he was called, obeyed and went out to a place he was going to receive as an inheritance; he went out, not knowing where he was going" (Hebrews 11:8). Abraham had never seen the Promised Land and knew nothing of its desirable characteristics, yet he strangely obeyed, not on the basis of his desire but on his knowledge of God.

I've seen this at work in my own life many times. Let me give you a recent example. I was working on this chapter when the Lord interrupted my ministry by a severe attack of cellulitis. My left leg was swollen and very red, and I had a high temperature. My left ankle had an abscess. I visited the emergency room and ended up in the hospital for six weeks and then had four weeks of physical rehabilitation so I could learn how to walk again. During those early weeks, the pain prohibited my reading books (for some inexplicable reason, I could read the Bible).

Lying there day after day, I prayed constantly: *Lord, my wisdom is finite and I have no way of knowing what Your ultimate purpose is in this illness. But I trust Your love and I know Your wisdom is infinite. Whatever result You want to bring from this incapacity, I praise You that on the other side, after I am well, You will bring something far better for me than if I had continued traveling and teaching.*

God's goal for me was a new paradigm. I was forbidden to drive and found myself with several free months in which I could write (hence, this book). As I plunged into writing, my prayers had a new sense of the reality of what God was doing. I realized that God is infinite, not only in wisdom but also in His attention. He is attending to DNA, babies, the paths of galaxies, and political upheavals with the same individual care that He attends to me!

THE OBJECT OF OUR FAITH

The ending of Hebrews 11:1 says that faith is the proof of what is not seen. It is not merely proof for us, the children of God; it is also proof for the world. It is our opportunity to exhibit Christ to the world through acting on what we see in the invisible. The world cannot see the unseen, so it is our privilege to establish that sense of reality for unsuspecting observers.

Faith cannot exist without an object. God went to much trouble to provide us with that object: the incarnated Christ. We don't need to struggle in a vacuum to know what God is like; the record is there for us to know and study. Seeing the unseen begins with Christ. Faith teaches us, "Whatever you do, in word or in deed, do everything in the name of the Lord Jesus, giving thanks to God the Father through Him" (Colossians 3:17).

CHAPTER FOUR

THE PATHWAY TO FAITH

*The Son of God, Jesus Christ . . . did not become "Yes and
no"; on the contrary, "Yes" has come about in Him. For
every one of God's promises is "Yes" in Him. Therefore the
"Amen" is also through Him for God's glory through us.*

2 CORINTHIANS 1:19-21

STEP 1: FACTOR THE WORD OF GOD INTO YOUR PRAYERS

The Holy Spirit makes us aware of Christ's working for us and
in us, but in order to take full advantage of the Spirit's work, we
must follow the biblical pathway to faith clearly set out in
Scripture. Jesus demonstrated the first step in that pathway,
quoting Deuteronomy 8:3. His rebuttal to Satan's first temptation placed the temptation in God's framework, not in Satan's:
"It is written: 'Man must not live on bread alone but on every
word that comes from the mouth of God'" (Matthew 4:4). The
Word of God was Jesus' food. God promised,

My word that comes from My mouth
will not return to Me empty,
but it will accomplish what I please,
and will prosper in what I send it to do. (ISAIAH 55:11)

The psalmist praised God's Word as being pure, like refined silver (see Psalm 12:6). In a later psalm, the writer proclaimed, "I will listen to what God will say" (85:8). In listing the spiritual armor of the Christian, Paul named the Word of God "the sword of the Spirit" (Ephesians 6:17). We do not use the Bible as an amulet; we cannot quote it as a superstitious charm. But by immersing ourselves in it, we are learning to think like God thinks. We are factoring in those aspects that will make us grow upward and move forward in Christlikeness—in the process of entelechy.

Not everyone who hears the message of Christ accepts it (see Hebrews 4:2). Satan lies eagerly waiting to snatch away "the word about the kingdom" (Matthew 13:19). This Matthew passage warns us Satan is watching for those who do not understand God's message; they are the seed sown on the hard soil of the path.

STEP 2: SEEK THE WILL OF GOD

The second step in the pathway to faith is to pray according to God's will. Jesus told His disciples, "My food is to do the will of Him who sent Me and to finish His work" (John 4:34). Jesus instructed us to seek first the kingdom of God and His righteousness (see Matthew 6:33). A time came when I decided to try that. I had been struggling with the meaning of the Sermon on the Mount and decided to rearrange my prayer list so that all of it reflected some work that would bring God's kingdom. I avoided praying about my personal problems, except in the way that they might affect the kingdom. I was startled to see how immediately the answers came! Not only that, but I found God attending to my personal problems in ways I did not even ask for: "All these things will be provided for you" (Matthew 6:33).

In disputing with the Jews, Jesus informed them, "If anyone wants to do His will, he will understand whether the teaching is from God or if I am speaking on My own" (John 7:17). Note that we must *want* to do God's will. When I realized this, it triggered in me a deep desire to please my Creator in His purposes for me.

HAVE PATIENCE

The psalmist said, "Commit your way to the LORD; trust in Him, and He will act" (Psalm 37:5). It may become an effort to discern God's will. Many times I have wanted to pray for something specific, but I realized I must "commit my way to the Lord." I did not voice the prayer request for weeks, struggling to make sure that it was actually God's will. I prayed, *Father, the deepest desire of my life is to please You, so I ask You to so direct my prayer that it will be in line with Your preordained will for my life.* Sometimes I would know immediately (for example, Scripture tells us that God wants to glorify His Son), but often the certainty of God's will did not instantly appear. God is working into our lives the factors of entelechy that will fit us for an eternity—never changing—with Christ.

God said through Jeremiah, "You will seek Me and find Me when you search for Me with all your heart" (29:12-13). In John 7 we are told to *want* to do God's will; here we're told to *search* for God. We have an active role in realizing God's purpose in creation and redemption. John made it clear: "This is the confidence we have before Him: whenever we ask anything according to His will, He hears us" (1 John 5:14).

TRUST GOD'S PROMISES

God seems to go out of His way to assure us in His promises. In James 5:15-16, He promises to hear the prayer for the sick. This is not a guarantee of immortality but of preservation (perhaps through healing) for the purpose of usefulness to God. Another faithful promise is, "You will receive power when the Holy Spirit has come upon you" (Acts 1:8). God does not impart power carelessly. His eye is constantly on our spiritual development, on our entelechy.

The strongest affirmation of God's good purposes for us occurs in 2 Corinthians 1:19-20:

> The Son of God, Jesus Christ . . . did not become "Yes and no"; on the contrary, "Yes" has come about in Him. For every one of God's promises is "Yes" in Him. Therefore the "Amen" is also through Him for God's glory through us.

That misunderstood word *amen* is virtually untranslatable. It certainly is not a sign-off for our prayers. *Amen* is one of the strongest affirmations in the Hebrew language. It is translated "verily" and "truly" and means "So be it." Christ in us is the strongest affirmation of the glory of God that we can share. "Moving a mountain" is the work of God, which is not accomplished by giants of the faith but by the simplest genuine belief (the size of a mustard seed).

FAITH PROVIDES ASSURANCE

When we live by faith, we are assured of God's outcome, and this produces in us a life of confidence. While facing outflanking armies, Jehoshaphat declared, "He has only human strength, but we have the LORD our God to help us and to fight our battles" (2 Chronicles 32:8). Paul assured the Corinthians, "We have this kind of confidence toward God through Christ: not that we are competent in ourselves to consider anything as coming from ourselves, but our competence is from God" (2 Corinthians 3:4-5). This is why God's power was perfected in Paul's weakness (see 12:9). The author of Hebrews spoke of drawing near to God in full assurance because "Christ was faithful as a Son over His household, whose household we are if we hold on to the courage and the confidence of our hope" (3:6). The same writer later encourages us not to throw away our confidence (see 10:35).

Job's faith, so often maligned, reoccurs again and again in his various discourses:

Even if He kills me, I will hope in Him. (13:15)

I know my living Redeemer,
and He will stand on the dust at last.
Even after my skin has been destroyed,
yet I will see God in my flesh. (19:25-27)

He knows the way I have taken; when He has tested me, I will emerge
as pure gold. (23:10)

Examples of enduring faith under trial emerge again and again throughout the Scriptures: Jehoshaphat (see 2 Chronicles

20:12), Elijah (see James 5:16-18), Daniel (see Daniel 6:23), the centurion whose slave was sick (see Matthew 8:10-11,13), the two blind men (see Matthew 9:27-29), the sinner at Simon's table (see Luke 7:50), and Paul (see Acts 27:25). These people did not have all the written promises we have today, yet they persisted in true faith under adverse circumstances. Their faith became the examples God recorded for the edification and instruction of New Testament saints and also for us.

Consider the following Old Testament promises:

All the Lord's ways show faithful love and truth to those who keep His covenant and decrees. (PSALM 25:10)

Take delight in the LORD, and He will give you your heart's desires. (PSALM 37:4)

Commit your activities to the LORD and your plans will be achieved. (PROVERBS 16:3)

The promises in the New Testament are even more staggering:

Keep asking, and it will be given to you. Keep searching, and you will find. Keep knocking, and the door will be opened to you. For everyone who asks receives, and the one who searches finds, and to the one who knocks, the door will be opened. (MATTHEW 7:7-8)

Remember, I am with you always, to the end of the age. (MATTHEW 28:20)

Look, I am sending you what My Father promised. (LUKE 24:49)

God's promises have a point. Hebrews reminds us that "He who promised is faithful" (Hebrews 10:23). God does not make an empty promise. Paul, trained by Pharisees, knew these promises, and he called on God continually, as evidenced by his ministry.

FROM GOD, NOT EFFORT

Faith does not depend on our own efforts; it is an emanation from God as a fruit of the Spirit (see Galatians 5:22). But we can ask for it. Jesus promised, "If you remain in Me and My words remain in you, ask *whatever you want* and it will be done for you" (John 15:7, emphasis added). God is the author of not only our salvation but also all Christlikeness, which He grows in us. The Spirit imparts to us an unmistakable sense that God is bending His ear to us as we pray to Him.

It is always faith that accomplishes divine involvement in response to a human prayer. "In Christ Jesus neither circumcision nor uncircumcision accomplishes anything; what matters is faith working through love" (Galatians 5:6). It is not observance but faith. "Faith, if it doesn't have works, is dead by itself" (James 2:17). Although faith is not outward, it produces outward results. It may not be obvious to others; the only way they can see our faith is in what it produces. "The intense prayer of the righteous is very powerful. . . . [Elijah] prayed earnestly that it would not rain, and for three years and six months it did not rain on the land. Then he prayed again, and the sky gave rain and the land produced its fruit" (5:16-18). Elijah's prayer demonstrates that the answer is not a result of psychological suggestion.

NO EARTHLY PRECONDITIONS

Wealth and power are not preconditions of faith (see Zephaniah 3:12). God gives faith to the humble. Zephaniah tells us that this "meek and humble people" will trust in the name of Yahweh, which in the New Testament becomes trust in the name of Jesus (see John 15:16). In the parable of the rich man and Lazarus (see Luke 12:16-20), the outcast Lazarus went to Abraham's bosom. In 1 Corinthians 1:26-31, Paul makes a big issue of the power of the humble. James says that God chose the poor in the world to be rich in faith (see 2:5-6).

Paul reminds us that although Jesus was rich, He became poor (see 2 Corinthians 8:9). One only has to note the place of His birth, His choice of disciples, and where He chose to minister to see what is, for God, an almost incredible humility. If anyone could have chosen earthly honors, it was God incarnate. He was deliberately untrained in the schools of this world. Paul, trained in the rabbinical schools, had to desert his background to be serviceable to God.

The pathway to faith is accessible to anyone who wants it. The psalmist invites us to trust in God at all times, to pour out our heart before Him (see Psalm 62:8). Paul passes on the information that "the message is near you, in your mouth and in your heart" (Romans 10:8). He also prayed that the Messiah might dwell in the Ephesians' hearts through faith (see Ephesians 3:16-17).

THINGS THAT FAITH PRODUCES

The pathway to faith produces maturity. Maturity comes through unity in the faith. Unity can derive only from the Head of the church (see Matthew 23:8-10). Paul, when discussing spiritual offices to build up the body of Christ, said that we would all attain "unity in the faith and in the knowledge of God's Son, growing into a mature man with a stature measured by Christ's fullness" (Ephesians 4:13). In his letter to the Corinthian church, he emphasized that if one member suffered, all would suffer. A mature person has many interacting parts. Our physical bodies illustrate this spiritual truth. For example, when I had cellulitis, the pain was in my leg, but the fever was in my body.

Life in Christ is a life of warfare, protected by the shield of faith (see Ephesians 6:16). Paul taught the Thessalonian church that faith and love are armor in our warfare (see 1 Thessalonians 5:8), and he urged Timothy to "fight the good fight for the faith" (1 Timothy 6:12).

If we stay on it, the pathway to faith will grow brighter and brighter: "The path of the righteous is like the light of dawn, shining brighter and brighter until midday" (Proverbs 4:18). Paul praised the Thessalonians because their faith was flourishing (see 2 Thessalonians 1:3). Growth is a command; we are to progress ever upward and forward. We are to "grow in the grace and knowledge of our Lord and Savior Jesus Christ" (2 Peter 3:18: entelechy in practice).

The pathway of faith produces other virtues: joy and peace (see Romans 15:13) and joy and salvation (see 1 Peter 1:8-9). Our joy is not achieved by bigger houses or better jobs; it is a concomitant to our ever-growing faith in Christ (entelechy in progress).

The end of the road is in sight as we progress on our path. Jesus completed His work (see John 17:4; 19:30). Paul counted his life of no value in comparison with finishing his course (see Acts 20:24; 2 Timothy 4:7-8). Paul told the Corinthians, "When the perfect comes, the partial will come to an end. . . . For now we see indistinctly, as in a mirror, but then face to face. Now I know in part, but then I will know fully, as I am fully known" (1 Corinthians 13:10,12). I have often heard someone say, "When I get to heaven, I've got some questions for God." However, I am quite certain that when I see the Lord Jesus, I will have no questions. My eyesight will be perfect.

CHAPTER FIVE

LEARNING TO SEE

*By [Christ] everything was created, in heaven and on
earth, the visible and the invisible, whether thrones or
dominions or rulers or authorities — all things have been
created through Him and for Him. He is before all things,
and by Him all things hold together.*

COLOSSIANS 1:16-17

SEEING THE SUPERIORITY OF THE SPIRITUAL

Believers have two sets of faculties: the physical and the spiritual. Primary with most of us is the physical. Nearly every activity we engage in involves the body: making a living, cooking the meals, walking down the street, smelling the roses, and on and on as our body utilizes as much as we can of our physical being. For all these necessary activities, God equipped us with an extraordinary set of senses and equipment.

This equipment is remarkable in that all the organs, hormones, senses, and innumerable other parts of our bodies have a function that is complete in itself. We *like* to eat, to smell, and to walk with abandon wherever we like, but these faculties all work together in an incredibly complex and complicated way. Nearly every activity of the body involves related nerves, organs, or parts. The taste buds work interactively with the olfactory nerves. The digestive system has a remarkable number of inter-acting parts, each of which must perform its function on cue. Even climbing the stairs is a marvelously complicated act.

Yet, in God's sight the spiritual is far greater and more fun-damental to our basic being than the physical. A spiritual God created baryons, human beings, solar systems, and galaxies. I suspect that in Eden, Adam and Eve were accustomed to serving spiritual purposes with their bodies. The martyrs who gave their lives for Christ gave their physical bodies to serve spiritual pur-poses. Most likely the great saints and prayer warriors of Christian history thought of themselves as primarily spiritual persons.

For most of us in the comfort of our modern world, think-ing *primarily* spiritually is a far reach, a difficult attainment. We *perform* our various Christian duties — periodic prayer, church attendance, intermittent witnessing, and so forth — and may even take pride in the "great Christians" we are, but most of our thinking and doing has its base in the physical.

In contrast, in the spiritual person, *every* thought and act springs from a consciousness of the unseen. The spiritual person doesn't simply hear the preacher; he or she searches for God's application of the message to his or her life. Reading the Bible is an encounter with true life.

The word of God is living and effective and sharper than any two-edged sword, penetrating as far as to divide soul, spirit, joints, and marrow; it is a judge of the ideas and thoughts of the heart. (HEBREWS 4:12)

I have two psychiatrist friends who are also committed Christians. They tell me that the spiritual outlook greatly affects the mental and physical condition of the patient. A serving and happy Christian seldom has mental hang-ups (although this has exceptions). On the other hand, a morose, sour Christian develops a self-defensive neurosis that is difficult to cure. I speak yearly to a large Christian counseling organization and am amazed at how a spiritual approach to patients' problems often brings about mental health.

Only Jesus exhibited the perfect integration of the physical and the spiritual. Without money or worldly position, He often attended meals that were large and well attended. (I became certain that Jesus enjoyed eating and that it was always right eating.) Jesus exhibited patience with slow-learning disciples, made long walks (Galilee was eighty miles north of Judea), and had a model physical life. Yet from all His teaching, no one can question the depth of His spirituality. The various circumstances of His development (what Aristotle called the "matter") combined to make a long overall structure of His life (Aristotle's "form") perfect to lead up to His consummate work, our redemption. The life of Christ was perfect entelechy in every stage. In Jesus, the spiritual was perfect and, consequently, the physical was perfect.

SEEING GOD'S DESIRE FOR OUR COOPERATION

God controls all circumstances, but in His respect for His creation, He sometimes allows our vagaries to play out so that His intervention at the proper time will have a teaching function for us. God maintains His sovereignty by controlling our use (and

His use above us) of circumstances.

For example, God was not pleased with Hitler, but He engineered a new nation from the Holocaust. God did not induce my cellulitis, but He produced within me a deeper understanding of His infinite wisdom through the long hours in a hospital bed, and my love for Him grew exponentially. God uses our circumstances to demonstrate His sovereignty in complex ways beyond our understanding. We stray constantly, yet He remains in control.

God is absolutely sovereign, but He also wants reciprocity. Without compelling our love, He uses various trials to move us to closer dependence on Him. Jesus extended invitations: "Come to Me, all of you who are weary and burdened, and I will give you rest" (Matthew 11:28). By definition, an invitation can be accepted or rejected. The rich young ruler abandoned Jesus; Peter followed Him. The Lord used the ruler's rejection to teach the disciples about the danger of riches, and Peter preached the Pentecost sermon.

God is always in control, and He wants us to work together with Him. We are not robots; we are partners with God (see 1 Corinthians 3:9). One of the many reasons He chose us was for us to participate in His work. This shows us more of His glory.

SEEING GOD'S "ABOVENESS"

We must never forget that God is infinitely above us. Our finiteness is one of the ways He encloses us in a box: An ant cannot "see" the Empire State Building, as his world is too limited. Our world too is limited by our size. Size means nothing to Infinity. While our vision is limited to our background, culture, and heredity, God fully comprehends the miniscule and the macroscopic, the distant galaxies and the quarks. He has no limitations of any kind.

Our limitations—our box—confine us to what is presently permissible for us. Our very language inhibits the size and depth of our understanding of God. For example, human language at present cannot reconcile how God can be transcendent (see Isaiah 57:15) and immanent (see Ephesians 1:23) at the same time. In our new heavenly bodies, we will not be limited by our present vocabulary. Concepts that seem at present to be contradictory will be comprehensible with a new larger language and larger conceptual equipment.

Despite our human limitations, God wants us to see the unseen, which means there are enormous vistas available to our spiritual sight if we look in the right direction. The spiritual world was real to Augustine, Martin Luther, and John Calvin, and that vision is available to us today.

SEEING GOD'S ONENESS

One of the unseen truths missed by much of the world is the oneness of God. The three monotheistic religions—Judaism, Islam, and Christianity—all claim Abraham as their father. This is striking in that he is the Christian's example of New Testament faith (see Romans 4:9,16-22). The first two religions disclaim Christianity's monotheism because they say we have three Gods.

Both Testaments emphasize the oneness of God (see Deuteronomy 6:4; Mark 12:29). God put this first because He knew that our conceptual apparatus, conditioned by language, would have difficulty in comprehending Three in One. We are limited in our thought life by mathematics. We're also limited by words that cannot be translated. For example, no other language that I know has an exact equivalent for the word *like*. In Spanish, we have to say, "It pleases me." In many Oriental languages, the word for *sin* carries with it an additional connotation of shame. This supplements the concept of sin being against God with an additional connotation of social embarrassment. Sometimes missionaries have to search for ways to demonstrate that people are primarily sinners against God, not merely factors in a social environment.

Our understanding of God and His oneness is inhibited by the limitations of language. Let me explain. I have always enjoyed learning languages because each language carries for me some additional connotations of what God is. In the Romance languages, worship is based on the idea of adoration of God, whereas in German, worship conveys showing honor to God (the word *Verehrung*, not *Gottesdienst*, which applies to a service of worship). The Hebrew word imparts the idea of bowing down or prostrating oneself before God. The Greek word implies doing reverence to (I enjoy the older, original meaning of this word: to kiss toward, which implies strong affection). As I have worshipped in different countries, I have found more depth from country to country because each talked about worship in ways I had not thought of. Different languages have deepened my worship.

But I am limited in my worship because I know so few languages. In heaven, we shall know fully (see 1 Corinthians 13:12). Evidently our eternal language will embody all the different concepts embodied in our earthly language. It will be enlarged to include fully the divine concepts, and we will understand much that was a mystery to us on earth.

God emphasizes His oneness first so that our approach to Him will not be one-sided. We must first know that the three Persons are one, single, alike in essence (for want of a better word). All the attributes of God are inherent completely in each member of the Godhead. Theologians speak of the Oneness in Threeness as *perichoresis*—in Latin, *circumincession*—which refers to the interpenetration of the three Persons or the fact that each is present in the other. But our current language is feeble, and with our new heavenly language we shall not be limited to thinking only in ciphers. Three in One will make sense with a broader and perfect mind. We will see that Three in One is the same as One in Three.

Knowing the various functions of the Persons helps us, without dividing God, to understand how God can be Three in One. For example, the Father is Potter, Protector, and Stimulator of our growth in Christ. The Son is Creator (see Colossians 1:16; Hebrews 1:12), Savior, King, and much more. The Spirit is our Indweller, Infiller, and Helper in realizing the purposes of the Father in us. Still, in some way, all three Persons work together in all the various functions. (The diagram on page 54 illustrates this interrelatedness.)

That each member of the Trinity points to the other two indicates that God, within His unity, is also *otherness*. The Father tells us to listen to His Beloved Son (see Luke 9:35) and chooses to spread His love abroad by the Holy Spirit (see Romans 5:5). The Son glorifies the Father (see John 17:4) and promises another Counselor who will teach them (see John 14:26). The Spirit makes us cry, "*Abba*, Father!" (Galatians 4:6), and the Spirit testifies about the Son (see 1 John 15:26).

Only a God who is in Himself otherness would have a motive to create intelligent humanity who, as other than God, can love Him with the pure love He has within Himself. God did not create all this otherness after creation. He was otherness prior to all creation.

Likewise, God did not become love after He made all of us

to have someone to love; He was love in Himself before all creation. The wonder of this was brought home to me when my daughter and I made a computerized list of all the times the Qur'an mentions love. I discovered that, in many instances, love is conditional; Allah will love you *if* you do this or that (Sura 2:190; 3:31-32,154; 4:36; 5:64,87; and many others). When I saw this, I turned to my daughter and exclaimed, "Aren't you glad that John 3:16 tells us that God is love?"

In addition to otherness and love, the One-in-Three has the quality of humility. Each member of the Trinity *wants* us to look at the other two. Even Jesus asserted that He was "gentle and humble in heart" (Matthew 11:29). Incidentally, a prayer I pray for Christian leaders is that (1) God will give them spiritual knowledge and (2) they will realize that their tiny portion of knowledge is inconsequential in relation to God's inexhaustible, infinite knowledge and they will be humble, knowing how much they *don't* know. The following diagram illustrates these concepts:

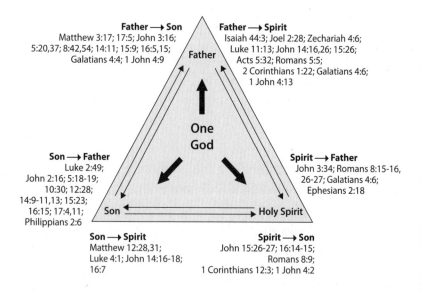

Father → Son
Matthew 3:17; 17:5; John 3:16;
5:20,37; 8:42,54; 14:11; 15:9; 16:5,15;
Galatians 4:4; 1 John 4:9

Father → Spirit
Isaiah 44:3; Joel 2:28; Zechariah 4:6;
Luke 11:13; John 14:16,26; 15:26;
Acts 5:32; Romans 5:5;
2 Corinthians 1:22; Galatians 4:6;
1 John 4:13

Father

One God

Son → Father
Luke 2:49;
John 2:16; 5:18-19;
10:30; 12:28;
14:9-11,13; 15:23;
16:15; 17:4,11;
Philippians 2:6

Spirit → Father
John 3:34; Romans 8:15-16,
26-27; Galatians 4:6;
Ephesians 2:18

Son

Holy Spirit

Son → Spirit
Matthew 12:28,31;
Luke 4:1; John 14:16-18;
16:7

Spirit → Son
John 15:26-27; 16:14-15;
Romans 8:9;
1 Corinthians 12:3; 1 John 4:2

The otherness and love of the Holy Trinity wanted to add further otherness by creating humanity. In that desire, God knew that humankind would fall and that all His revelation would be construed legalistically. In spite of the admonitions of the prophets and holy men to interpret the Law spiritually,[2] God knew that ultimately the only convincing revelation would be the enfleshment of one member of the Trinity. The issue became "Which member of the Trinity should God incarnate in order to reveal His true nature and purposes?"

As Father, God is the Giver: "God so loved the world that He gave" and "Every generous act and every perfect gift is from above, coming down from the Father of lights" (James 1:17; see also Luke 11:3; Acts 17:25; Romans 6:23). It would be within His nature as Father to give either the Son or the Spirit.

On the other hand, if God sent us the Spirit, we humans would have conceptual difficulty comprehending how Spirit could be flesh. If His humanity were genuine, people would see Him eating, drinking, sleeping, simply doing the things humans have to do by their nature. His followers could only ask, "Is He flesh, or is He Spirit?" So the wisdom of the Godhead ruled out the Father and the Spirit as One to become genuinely human.

Obviously, this left only the Son. Jesus, as God, knew that His incarnation would entail unbelievable humility and that the divine plan would involve Calvary as the ultimate fulfillment of the Law. He willingly created the universe and us in the knowledge of the awesome sacrifice His incarnation would require.

This is why our songs have been about Him for two thousand years. Jesus represents all that the Godhead is for our comprehension. If you wish to know what the Father is like, look at Jesus; if you want to know what the Spirit is like, look to Jesus. Our access to God is in Jesus' name. This is why the Lord Jesus

Christ must be, for all of us, the ultimate and final revelation of God.

CHAPTER SIX

PROBING REALITY

The LORD said,
"Should I hide from Abraham what I am about to do?"
GENESIS 18:17

Indeed, the Lord GOD does nothing without revealing His
counsel to His servants the prophets.
AMOS 3:7

I've mentioned that when I become fully conscious of faith, a sense of reality of God's presence and work in our lives permeates my prayers. This is so important. I've been able to identify seven factors that infuse my prayers of faith and provide me with a sense of reality as I pray. Let's look at each of these.

1. A STRONG SENSE OF THE HOLY SPIRIT'S MEDIATION (SEE EPHESIANS 5:18)

I have a strong sense of the presence of the Holy Spirit mediating my prayer to the Father as I pray. Jesus promised to send another Helper (see John 14:16). The word for "another" here is *allos*, which refers to another of the same kind (as Jesus); the other word for "another" is *heteros*, which is another of a different kind, as in Romans 7:23 (another law of a different kind). But our Helper is of the essence of Jesus Himself. His help is as strong as it would be if Jesus Himself were praying the prayer.

The Holy Spirit informs our prayer in many ways. He empowers us (see Acts 1:8), glorifies (regenerates) us (see 2 Corinthians 3:17-18), relates to us as God the Father (see Galatians 4:6-7), helps (or comforts) us (see John 14:16-17), reveals things to us (see Luke 2:26), teaches us (see John 14:16), sanctifies us (see 2 Thessalonians 2:13), and has many more activities on our behalf. He even intercedes for us (see Romans 8:26).

The apostles fulfilled the Great Commission by evangelizing Judea, Samaria, the entire northern African coast, all of the southern European coast, and much of the then-known Middle East. They did this in the power and direction of the Holy Spirit. Jesus had said that the apostles would do greater works than He (see John 14:12). Such a grand claim must have startled the disciples. Jesus evangelized only the tiny nation of Israel, but, under the leadership of the Spirit, the apostles evangelized the entire then-known world.

The Spirit's work is so important that we are to be filled with Him (see Ephesians 5:18), as the apostles were at Pentecost. Small wonder that Jude instructs us to pray in the Spirit (see Jude 20). The Bible goes out of its way to emphasize the importance of the Holy Spirit in our prayers.

2. A COMMITMENT TO PRAYING IN THE MIND OF CHRIST (SEE 1 CORINTHIANS 2:16)

We are to pray in the mind of Christ. It is the work of the Holy Spirit to bear witness to Christ (see John 15:26). The work of Jesus in His incarnation included healing, teaching, and, above all, proclaiming the coming of the kingdom of God. We have seen how the Spirit led to Africa, Europe, and the Middle East. The apostles healed, taught, and brought the kingdom in a broad geographical area.

Throughout the book of Acts, we find the apostles in constant movement. They proclaimed the gospel successfully in unexpected places. The Holy Spirit directed Paul to Europe, to win a following in Cypress, and enabled him to survive a shipwreck. We cannot predict the direction and movement of the Spirit of God. Rather than build a super-church in Jerusalem (which would be the normal expectation), we find the apostles working in Antioch, Thessalonica, the island of Cyprus, and all the way to Rome.

Always their message centered on Christ and Him crucified — not an appealing call, yet following the Holy Spirit, they remained faithful to the message of the gospel, as difficult as it might have been. Persecution inevitably followed. Instead of acclaim for their courage, the apostles endured beatings and imprisonment, and Christ became Lord of innumerable people as the apostles and other witnesses persisted in a hard calling.

Again and again, Christ encouraged them through His Spirit. On occasion, He appeared to Paul to bolster him through much more than we endure today. Did Paul pray as he clung to the shattered wood of the shipwreck? He knew that Jesus did not say, "I will be with you" (a promise to look forward to) but I *am* with you (a present Christ in very strange circumstances).

The New Testament records always keep Christ at the center of their message.

3. A STRONG SENSE of PROGRESSION, UPWARD and FORWARD (SEE PHILIPPIANS 3:13-14)

Paul wrote, "I press on toward the goal for the prize of the upward call of God in Christ Jesus" (Philippians 3:14, ESV). Christianity always looks upward and forward. This becomes especially obvious in Paul's prayers in Ephesians. Note the surging upward movement in his prayers in the first and third chapters:

> *Since I heard about your faith in the Lord Jesus and your love for all the saints, I never stop giving thanks for you as I remember you in my prayers. I pray that the God of our Lord Jesus Christ, the glorious Father, would give you a spirit of wisdom and revelation in the knowledge of Him. I pray that the eyes of your heart may be enlightened so you may know what is the hope of His calling, what are the glorious riches of His inheritance among the saints, and what is the immeasurable greatness of His power to us who believe, according to the working of His vast strength.* (1:15-21)

> *I bow my knees before the Father, from whom every family in heaven and on earth is named, that according to the riches of his glory he may grant you to be strengthened with power through his Spirit in your inner being, so that Christ may dwell in your hearts through faith — that you, being rooted and grounded in love, may have strength to comprehend with all the saints what is the breadth and length and height and depth, and to know the love of Christ that surpasses knowledge, that you may be filled with all the fullness of God.*

*Now to him who is able to do far more abundantly than all that we
ask or think, according to the power at work within us, to him be glory
in the church and in Christ Jesus throughout all generations, forever
and ever. Amen.* (3:14-21, ESV)

Each of these prayers contains an enormous amount of
information about Christ and even about prayer itself. Paul ends
with a magnificent doxology. It is hard to believe that he *dic-
tated* this grand theology in such flow as these prayers exhibit.
Each segment of his prayers builds on the last, leading up to the
mountaintop praise at the end. Such praise is appropriate,
according to the leading of the Spirit, for such gigantic prayers.

When I am gripped by the sense of reality of God's presence
and work in our lives, He seems to move me in a prayer that is
always moving forward (although not on Paul's scale). My prayer
list starts with mundane matters (my family and friends), then
to the movement of the Spirit in this country, and then to the
church and the kingdom. I pray much about obstacles to the
kingdom and then pray for this country. My prayer continues
with missions agencies (when I name eleven agencies, I ask that
they be tokens of many other agencies around the world that I
do not know about). Then I pray for about fifty-three countries
in which persecution is severe and keep going with a number of
"kingdom bringers," people who I know are furthering the sovereignty of Christ. This is a rather long list, and because I am
praying for the coming of the kingdom, the remainder takes
most of the rest of my time, still always concentrating on the
coming kingdom. Often I realize I am praying about physical
needs in those various agencies, but the Holy Spirit seems to
impel me forward through the various lists.

Obviously we cannot approach the matchless prayers of

Paul. He was an apostle; we are disciples. We are to follow his example, not set a new one. His prayers are recorded for our instruction.

4. A DEEP, STRONG DESIRE TO PLEASE THE FATHER (SEE JOHN 8:29)

Several years ago, after a painful "no" answer from God to one of my prayers, I found myself on my face crying, "Father, I want desperately to please You." That prayer produced a new work in my prayer life. At the beginning of my prayer, I began crying out for the Spirit to help me know what kind of prayer would please the Father, especially what prayers would glorify Him. I have not achieved my goal, but my prayers go in a different direction now.

I attribute this to my praying for the leadership of the Spirit. Because prayer is incense, I ask that my "incense" be so pleasing to the Father that He will use it as a tool to accomplish His purposes.

Incense played a major role in the Old Testament offerings and sacrifices. In the New Testament, "we are the aroma of Christ to God among those who are being saved and among those who are perishing, to one a fragrance from death to death, to the other a fragrance from life to life" (2 Corinthians 2:15-16, ESV). The elders before the throne of the Lamb in Revelation held golden bowls full of incense, which are the prayers of the saints. So our prayer can be pleasing to God as incense for His use!

As beginners in this role of offering incense prayers to God, we start by knowing that we cannot ask for something foreign to the holiness of God. The more we develop our prayer lives, the more we will become sensitive to what pleases God, and the more we will want our prayers to be welcome in His holy presence.

I believe that God takes pleasure in our prayers, however juvenile and unworthy they might be. The tone of Matthew 7 and Luke 11 indicates that He *wants* us to pray. It is our joy to learn how to be pleasing to the Lord in our prayers. Prayer is conversation with God, and God's love indicates that He wants to converse with His beloved children. Both Matthew 7 and Luke 11 contain contrasts of a loving earthly father with the magnificent generosity of our heavenly Father. These two chapters indicate the disposition of a God who wants to give.

Since He is God in ineffable holiness, it should be our pleasure to want to please Him. It can be done, and with it comes inexpressible joy. *Tell* Him you want to please Him, and ask for directions on how to do it.

5. A STRONG SENSE THAT NOTHING IS IMPOSSIBLE WITH OMNIPOTENCE
(SEE MATTHEW 21:21)

When we request something in prayer, the last thing we should consider is the difficulty in carrying out an answer to our prayer. More than eight passages in the Bible emphasize God's attribute of omnipotence. When the disciples asked Jesus to teach them to pray, He usually answered with an affirmation of God's power. Jesus used the cursing of the fig tree to underline this significant point (see Matthew 21:18-21).

Elijah's faith was so monumental that he had the people pour gallons of water on his sacrifice before the fire fell. Jesus often said, "Be it unto you according to your faith" (see Matthew

9:29). The only person to hesitate before the power of Jesus was Martha. She told Him, "Lord, by this time there will be an odor" (John 11:39, ESV). Most of the people healed by Jesus expected a "yes" answer.

We in this twenty-first century expect marvels on every side: telescopes that can see 13.7 billion light years away, medical marvels, and a technology giving us computers that can solve the most intricate equations. Yet we balk at asking God to do the "impossible." God told Abraham three thousand years ago that nothing was impossible with Him.

To doubt God's omnipotence is to cast a shadow on the miracles of the Bible. Yet even today, with all our technology, we cannot still a hurricane or multiply loaves and fish. I tell my grandchildren frequently that the greatest thing I have learned in life is that *God is God.* Neither human imagination nor the direst circumstance is beyond infinity.

This young century hardly knows God as God. Our churches do not often emphasize prayer. Probably the greatest hindrance to a praying church lies in the failure to believe that God will do what He says He will do. Our prayer meetings often are simply a listing of the sick or a listing of the lost. One church I know has above every door, "My house shall be called a house of prayer" (Matthew 21:13, ESV). God, give us more!

6. CONCENTRATING THOUGHTS ENTIRELY ON GOD (SEE EPHESIANS 4:6)

Not only is God omniscient, He is also omni-attentive. Faith fosters a confidence that He hears us.

One of my personal failures is that I am not nearly as attentive as God wants me to be. Most people admit that their mind wanders or they get sleepy during prayer. This common failure interferes with the prayer we are trying to make. I pray that the Holy Spirit will help me maintain attention to His direction as He leads me onward and upward.

Contrast this with the fact that God not only knows all things, including our thoughts, but also keeps His attention constantly on what we are saying or thinking, even when we do not mean it or we are saying it absently. I have even had God provide a "yes" answer to a prayer I prayed without my mind on it! God's mercies are new every morning, and these include the fact that all prayer, conscious or unconscious, ascends as incense to Him. God's nobility rises far above our weakness. He hears far more than we can imagine.

We especially fail to thank Him for His untold number of blessings. Thanksgiving runs like a river throughout the book of Revelation. Years ago I asked God to help me become more aware of His various intended blessings, and I couldn't keep up! Finally I found myself praying, *Lord, I thank You for all these things I can name, but now I know that it is impossible to thank You for every one of Your blessings. I ask You to use my gratitude for the nameable and knowable blessings as tokens of my gratitude for all those other blessings that are unnamable and unknowable.*

Jesus is the only man who thought of God without a break. When Jesus was healing, He was praying; when He was teaching, He was praying; when He was fellowshipping with His disciples and others, He was praying. He was even praying when He was dealing with His enemies.

We are not capable of maintaining that kind of attention on God, but most of us could do much better than we actually accomplish. Prayer especially demands attention, and with the Spirit's help, we can improve our prayer lives with the right kind of discipline. This is one reason a quiet devotional time alone with the Lord becomes so helpful. Originally I was a night person. I came to life with the evening hours. But years ago I asked God to wake me up at the hour that would give Him time to communicate what He wanted to say to me and at an hour that would give me the sleep I needed. I woke up at three in the morning! I was surprised at how much more clearly I could hear from the Lord at that time and still function as though I'd had enough sleep. This practice has helped my thought discipline immensely. In the early hours there is little that distracts from the Lord, especially speaking through His Word.

I challenge you to try an early-morning quiet time to give the Holy Spirit the opportunity to broaden your vision and discipline your prayer time. It worked for me.

7. A SINCERE DESIRE FOR THE WILL OF GOD ABOVE PERSONAL WHIMS (SEE MATTHEW 6:10)

Most of the time I have confidence that my desires spring forth from God's desires. When He created us, He had a specific role for each of our lives that we are to fulfill. Our purpose is to discover why God created us and what He has in His great mind for this particular part of our lives.

First Corinthians 3:9 states that we are God's fellow workers. God did not need any of us to accomplish His purposes. He did not need the angels. But His nature as Trinity shows us that it gives Him pleasure to work together. In His infinite joy in creation, He wanted to create a race that enjoyed working with Him. His declaration that His creation was good hints at the joy creation gave Him. He declared that the creation of humans was "very good" (Genesis 1:31).

All the ramifications of the "very good" creation tell us that God receives joy when we accomplish His purpose for our particular creation. I frequently pray that the Holy Spirit will so enable me in carrying out God's plan for my day that, in the doing of God's will, I may share His co-joy (on my elementary level) in finishing or in doing what God had in mind for me on that day.

God is always active; He never slumbers. In turn, we, created in His likeness for His purposes, are to make "the best use of the time, because the days are evil" (Ephesians 5:16, ESV). Days may come when the best use of our time will include diversions to help us concentrate more easily. Jesus enjoyed days with Martha, Mary, and Lazarus. However, the best use of our time will not include dawdling or wasteful activities.

In short, God's purpose for our days will provide a satisfaction and joy that no worldly pleasure can match. The Creator knew what He was doing when He fashioned us, all for a purpose more satisfying to us than anything else in this world. When He redeemed us, He transported us into the world of His highest pleasures.

CHAPTER SEVEN

A CAVEAT

The secret counsel of the LORD is for those who fear Him.
PSALM 25:14

MUCH TO ACCOMPLISH

As I was finishing chapter 6, I was struck by how far short I fell from the ideal I was writing about. In fact, the Holy Spirit convicted me of how far I have to go in personally realizing everything in this book.

We are admonished to go to further depths after salvation:

Leaving the elementary message about the Messiah, let us go on to maturity, not laying again the foundation of repentance from dead works, faith in God, teaching about ritual washings, laying on of hands, the resurrection of the dead. (HEBREWS 6:1-2)

So many Christians remain at such an elementary level in their spiritual growth that great works for God remain outside their experience or ability. Hebrews tells us to mature spiritually, to move forward. This is especially true of prayer.

We are commanded to, after our initial salvation, "grow in the grace and knowledge of our Lord and Savior Jesus Christ" (2 Peter 3:18). From my experience in hundreds of evangelical churches and associations, few people are truly "growing in grace and knowledge of the Lord." The majority of church members seem to be satisfied that an initial profession and baptism earns them the right to be called Christian for the rest of their lives, with no further development or growth involved. For many, a public profession secures their position for eternity, and a profession of faith is little more than a social duty.

If you took everything I have written so far at face value, you, the reader, might become discouraged at how much we all have to do and that there is much left to accomplish in our churches and membership. Indeed, we do have much to accomplish with our lives if we truly believe 2 Peter 3:18.

Although the Lord began long ago impressing on me this sense of reality that so often grips me as I pray, I felt I needed to grade myself on the seven factors I listed in the previous chapter. I sincerely felt that I had reached about a B minus. I was not discouraged, as I realized that when the sense of reality started, my score was a D minus. So in the years of praying for more and more of the Holy Spirit, the Lord has taken me from D minus to B minus.

GOD WORKS IN PROCESS

This leads me to share an important concept that emerged early in my struggle: God works in process. Although I mentioned this in my book *From Heaven's View*, I want to reaffirm it for the reader of this book.

Jesus told this parable in Mark 4:26-29:

"The kingdom of God is like this," He said. "A man scatters seed on the ground; he sleeps and rises — night and day, and the seed sprouts and grows — he doesn't know how. The soil produces a crop by itself — first the blade, then the head, and then the ripe grain on the head. But as soon as the crop is ready, he sends for the sickle, because harvest has come."

This story has many meanings, but the one I want to extract is the concept that in our weakness, God works in process, sometimes very slowly. Jesus is pointing out that the only knowledge the farmer has for certain is the beginning of the process (the seed) and its end (the mature fruit). All through the growth process, the farmer can be aware of only certain indications of growth. He sleeps as normal. Those indications give him hope for the climax, the ripe grain.

Jesus said that the kingdom of God resembles His parable. Salvation is not merely an event, although it is an event. However, we should also view salvation as a continuing process.

Work out your own salvation with fear and trembling, for it is God who works in you, both to will and to work for his good pleasure. (PHILIPPIANS 2:12-13, ESV)

Because the seed is from God, only He gets credit for the mature grain. But during the growth process, the farmer must fertilize the seed, prune and weed, pray for rain, and be alert for pests — all the while watching hopefully for God's maturation of the crop. In the same way, our salvation is a process, requiring a real "workout," and we have a role in the working out of the process.

OUR ROLE in WORKING OUT the PROCESS

All Christians have to go through the process, and it requires exercise. I know too well about failures, times of temptation, and Satan's armies interfering at sensitive points. Like the farmer, we sleep and rise night and day, at times caught unaware of the wiles of the Enemy. Sometimes we become lethargic and sluggish in our struggle upward.

Take, for instance, the seven aspects mentioned in the previous chapter of the sense of reality I have experienced concerning God's presence and work in our lives. The first factor, the importance of the Holy Spirit's work, was the least conscious part of my struggle. I knew about the Holy Spirit's role mainly from preachers, plus the little I had read in books, yet it took a tense mission meeting for me to suddenly grasp, pray, and struggle to the point that there was nothing I could do except cry for the Spirit to do His powerful work. The Spirit worked mightily, and I remembered that Jesus told us we could do nothing without Him (see John 15:5). We ended that mission meeting with a glorious revival, but it did not come from humans; it came from God.

Desperation turns us to the right step. The Spirit Himself seems to shun the limelight. We ignore Him until we have to, and, as God, He is merciful and comes even when we neglect Him. Each reader could tell a similar story. The Spirit mercifully waits until we depend entirely on Him.

The second factor, praying with the mind of Christ, seems less neglected than the other six. We usually do not fail in our love, praise, and dependence on the person of Christ. The triune God wisely decided that Jesus be the Representative of the Godhead to show us what God is like. If you want to know what the Father is like, look at Jesus, His Revealer. To know the work of the Holy Spirit, look at the work of the Lord Jesus. Although we do not appreciate Jesus' glorious greatness, at least we sing about Him and praise Him in our services.

The sense of onward and upward movement, the third factor, may seem too nebulous to get hold of, yet when it happens, we get so caught up in praying that we are unaware of the passage of time. We are in the grip of the Holy Spirit leading us to fervent prayer. The first time I became consciously aware of it was on the campus of Southwestern Seminary in a time of campus revival. Nothing makes us long to move upward more than a revitalizing work of God. The onward progression was so powerful that we were enjoying numerous prayer meetings, and they were all a result of "pressing on." I have observed that revivals are usually short-lived.

Yet after the revival waned, I found myself in an "upward and onward" mode that never ceased. If you have never experienced a general spiritual awakening, pray for a personal arousing that will cause you to long for an ever-onward progression.

True prayer is exciting. I have been through a number of prayer meetings that were taken over by the Spirit of God. I am grateful that I have seen prayer meetings and private prayer pressed forward by the grasp of holiness in the prayers. This happens in not only corporate meetings but also private prayer, where we are gripped by a sense of reality. The sense of onward movement always expresses itself in an indescribable excitement, yet I have seen the sense of upwardness impeded by an exaggerated demonstrativeness on the part of a single person.

I have also been in prayer meetings in which the Spirit's upward and onward movement so frightened some of the participants that they deliberately tried to "calm it down." They were usually successful, for the Spirit's sensitivity is one of His most powerful characteristics. He comes and remains only where He is welcome. Where He is allowed to function, He accomplishes miracles — reconciliation of enemies and a fresh witness. I have seen this happen a number of times.

Most church members feel strongly about the Lord Jesus, but the Father stays in the background, which is a peculiar place for the Father of lights. We address our prayers to Him without comprehending His august, cosmic nature as Executive of the Trinity. He is our Preserver and Provider, yet we ignore Him and His high role.

I found a fresh sense of reality when, in an apparently humdrum prayer time, to instill life into it, I cried with all my heart, *Father, I seek Your pleasure with real desperation.* That cry turned a routine prayer time into a time of unusual personal revival, and I experienced the fourth factor: a strong desire to please the Father.

Many Christians also give lip service to the omnipotence of God, factor number five. We are like the New Testament Israelites, whose faith was so weak that it was necessary for Jesus to emphasize the power of God in much of His teaching on prayer. He said we could move mountains (see Matthew 21:21). He repeatedly said God was more willing to give than an earthly father (see 7:9-11).

Even the cosmic attributes of God may fall into a boring recitation. Omnipotence becomes one cipher in the lists we recite of God's attributes (God is omnipotent, omniscient, omnipresent, infinite, eternal, and so forth). Books have been written about the attributes of God, yet for many church members, they are only a litany of qualities that everybody knows. All the healings of Jesus illustrate omnipotence. How often it should be the center of our prayer meetings! It should also be at the center of our personal prayers.

The secular world—television, media, academia, and so forth—so preoccupy our attention that most of us find ourselves concentrating on the movie and television stars, the latest movie or television show, success in our careers, and on and on, so that God gets squeezed into a comer. We have little time for eternal matters. When we encounter a truly spiritual believer, we see that person as odd, a religious fanatic. The minds of Paul, John, and Peter were so given to Christ that they were persecuted for their faith. In the strangeness of these recent times, however, only believers in non-Western countries (Islamic, communist, and others) are victimized for their faith. A disturbing aspect is that in recent times, deeply devout Christians are marginalized in the West.

I was once sought out by a man who was looking for a "Spirit-filled person." (I had many personal failures, so this was really a coincidence.) But my heart broke as he recited his search for just one "Spirit-filled" person. All I could tell him was that Christ was at the center of my life—that was the only one of the seven factors that held water in my life at that time.

The fact of twenty-first-century Christian life is that although we fulfill our Christian duties (our church attendance and prayers are irregular), in the final analysis, God is on the periphery of our daily thinking. In most churches I know of, the Spirit-filled group constitutes a small minority. In the New Testament, we find a list of people who had God as the center of their lives. And they changed their world. Their thoughts were entirely concentrated on God—the sixth factor—and they made history.

The last of the seven factors of a sense of reality concerns our desire for the will of God. Think what a better world this would be if everyone in every church wanted the will of God above their personal whims!

Although my parents were devout Christians, the ambience of the little town and the little school I grew up in was that whatever will get you ahead is what matters in life. Although I was active in church, I caught that success-driven syndrome in my spirit. It is the supreme goal of most American Christians.

We had a deeply spiritual pastor, but I seldom heard a sermon on the will of God. It was not a preoccupation of the Christian world I knew, so it remained buried deep in my mind most of my life. Of the seven aspects of the sense of reality I have discussed, this was the last to occupy my mind. Even when my wife had cancer, my first concern in prayer was for her healing. We'd had fifty-eight and a half years together, and God had healed her many times. I expected Him to preserve her, even in the distress of widely spreading cancer.

But in persecuted countries, the will of God jumps to the uppermost level in the thinking of suffering Christians. They pay with imprisonment, beatings, ostracism, poverty, and even death for the will of God. I began encountering this strange attitude of persecuted Christians several years ago, and it became a problem for me. How could I not pray that God would heal my wife in the light of God's profound work around the world? The natural part of me always prayed for her preservation. Toward the obvious end, I prayed strongly that she would not suffer, and God answered that prayer magnificently. My wife had very little pain, even to the end.

After her death, I became immersed in a deep desire for the will of God and started praying in earnest for Him to have His way in the remaining years of my life. God answered that prayer in a renewed call to write on prayer. Part of the answer to that prayer was the calling to write this book.

The will of God is good. Even in my adjustment to my wife's absence, I have discovered that Romans 8:28 still holds true. None of us has immortality; death comes by the appointment of God, and it is universal. Thousands of believers around the world cling to Romans 8:28 in almost unbelievably trying circumstances.

My wife's death was painful to me—I cannot lie. The aching for her presence lasted months. But in church, a choir anthem, "A New Hallelujah," called me to place my new call to write on prayer in a place where God could work more plentifully. I'm not completely out of the doldrums, but I am writing with a new sense of onward progression.

So I cling to my B minus in all areas. I believe that even in the seventh aspect, I am up to a B minus. The sense of reality is paying off in many ways: in "yes" answers to prayers, in new insights that the Holy Spirit gives me as I continue to probe His Word, in new understandings of the triunity of God, in many new friendships with brothers and sisters who have taught me much, in frequent and penetrating insights from old friends, and, above all, in the divine comfort into which the Holy Comforter is lifting me deeper and deeper.

What about you? How well do you apply these seven factors to your life of faith? If you find yourself in a D-minus category, God will take you where you are and lift you up to at least a B minus. Real prayer is difficult, but the co-joy of the Lord will be the highest joy you have ever had.

Let's review the seven factors one last time. Apply these Scriptures to your prayers:

1. A strong sense of the Holy Spirit's mediation to the Father in all that I pray (see Ephesians 5:18). This works.

2. A commitment to praying in the mind of Christ (see 1 Corinthians 2:16). This has always worked for me.

3. A strong sense of progression, upward and forward (see Philippians 3:13-14). I sing "A New Hallelujah."

4. A deep, strong desire to please the Father (see John 8:29). This has become fresh in my prayers.

5. A strong sense that nothing is impossible with omnipotence (see Matthew 21:21). This points to all other of God's vast qualities.

6. Thoughts concentrated entirely on God (see Ephesians 4:6). He shows me constantly that His mercies are new every morning (see Lamentations 3:22-23).

7. A sincere desire for the will of God above personal whims (His will—see Matthew 6:10). His will is bringing new insights day by day.

CHAPTER EIGHT

REALIZING FAITH

Without faith it is impossible to please God, for the one who draws near to Him must believe that He exists and rewards those who seek Him.

HEBREWS 11:6

FOUR FACTORS TO NAIL DOWN

Faith is the "eyes" through which we see the unseen. In summary, and for a review, we have seen:

1. Faith is mediated through the Holy Spirit; it is a fruit of His presence.
2. With true faith comes a sense of reality (we can ask for this).
3. Faith is grown through knowledge of Christ.
4. The Word of God is necessary to develop faith (try memorizing God's promises in His Word).

Nail these four factors down, if you haven't already. The first is available to every believer, as the Holy Spirit is indwelling us. The second is imparted by the Spirit as we pray. The third requires assiduous study of the New Testament under the guidance of the Holy Spirit. The fourth requires real work. My personal faith has grown through the years as I worked at each of these four.

Hebrews 11:6 conveys that the faith God expects is propositional, not merely mystical. God *is*. He reveals Himself, and we exercise our minds to accept the Word of God. God is a rewarder of those who seek Him — that is fact. We seek first the Person of God, not things.

Having reached markers of spiritual maturity means that we do not have to repeat elementary aspects of faith. What are some indications of maturity? All the fruit of the Spirit (see Galatians 5:22-23) is decidedly present. Impatience is a sign of immaturity, and so are all the other opposites of the fruit. Our joy comes from concentration on God. With that, we can move mountains. Why would we want to move mountains (see Mark 11:23)? Because if we do not move the mountain — level the ground — we will have to climb it. A mountain many of us have had to surmount comes in the form of persecution (see John 15:20). How can we level the ground of persecution? By showing patience and love for our persecutors.

OBJECTIONS to FAITH

But then objections arise. The fiercest objection I heard was "I pray, but I don't feel I have connected with God." The absurdity of this objection lies in the fact that, as mentioned earlier, God is infinite in attention (an aspect of infinity largely ignored). On our small scale, it is difficult to take in much at all about infinity. God created the universe so enormous in order to give us a hint that He is greater than the reach of the most powerful telescope. Theologians are fond of talking about the immensity of God, but even the word *immensity* falls short of absolute limitlessness. To most of us, *immensity* suggests "great big" and could apply to Mount Everest. God is beyond any words human language can describe, even exhausting the exponentials we can attach to a number (10 to the nth power). God is much, much more than "great big." Whether we use macro numbers (billions of galaxies) or micro numbers (quarks and strings), God is beyond our feeble attempts at expression. He is beyond the quasars and most distant galaxies. He controls the quarks and cells of all existence.

And the miracle is that (beyond all imagination) He can pay attention to the activities of all supernovae as well as to our digestion and conversation. Nothing can escape the notice of Infinite Attention. While we do not understand this, Psalm 139 hints at a beyondness that neither the psalmist nor the most advanced astrophysicist can perceive: "I am with you always." We do not need to connect to God; He is always connected to us, even when we ignore Him or when we sin.

SENSING CONNECTION

So the problem lies in *our* sense of connectedness. Notice that I said *sense* of connectedness. God is connected to us, but we pray mindlessly, or we absently put Him out of our mind. God "hears" every prayer, but our prayers lack the intensity and earnestness of Elijah. (Elijah knew that the cutting, leaping, and screaming of the false priests could not be heard by a god who did not exist (reality). Elijah knew that God not only heard but could override buckets of water to ignite the sacrifice (again, reality). The one true God existed and rewarded the one who sought Him.

Every morning to "get connected" to God, I stand in my bathroom and acknowledge the unspeakable greatness of God. To be honest, the sense of connection is not always immediate. Many times I have to acknowledge what God has done for me and is currently doing. It may take minutes, but I keep at it until I am sure that I really am on track. Later in my prayer time, I have a period of praise before I begin my intercession in which I sometimes remember past undoubted actions of God. This praise time always includes many of His attributes and names.

I acknowledge my debt to the Holy Spirit, what He is currently doing, and ask God that my "24/7" be directed constantly by that omnipotent Spirit. I acknowledge that my sense of His reality within me continues through every thought and action. Some of the time, the Holy Spirit makes me actualize the reality of my redemption through concentrating on Calvary. Scriptures that God is currently using in me pop in and out of my mind. By the time I reach my office, which is my prayer room, not only is God's connectedness to me a felt reality but my personal connectedness with Him seems somehow ready to proceed.

I begin my prayer time, as I said, with a period of praise; sometimes I sing (it may be a good idea to carry your favorite choruses or hymns with you). This develops a perspective on who God is.

I have kept a prayer list for many years. This has often helped remind me of factors or agencies or persons I might forget. My personal prayer list is concerned almost entirely with the kingdom and will of God, including my prayers for myself and my family and friends. Depending on how much reality I sense as I progress, I often thank God ahead of time for hearing me. Time and again this has made my renewed thankfulness after a prayer answered with a "yes" more meaningful.

Then I spend some time in the Old Testament, some time in the Gospels (including Acts), and some time in the letters (including Revelation). Many people ignore the use of the Bible in their prayers, but my prayer list is peppered with various Scriptures I can use in different circumstances. Quoting Scripture to God is not an amulet; it should not become superstition. All I am doing when I refer to a Scripture, look one up, or quote one from memory is learning to think in the pattern in which God thinks.

You may object and say, "But that takes too much time." That depends on how eagerly you want God's action in your life for that day. The more time you spend in thinking His thoughts by means of His Word, the more familiar you become with the actions of the Holy Spirit in your prayer time and your day. Sometimes it helps to take a whole chapter or section of the Bible and seek to apply each verse to your current circumstances or whatever you are praying for.

I have mentioned that occasionally I need to pray about a particular item for weeks or even months. When I do that, a time usually arrives when God breaks through with a renewed sense of reality that the time is right for a "yes" answer. Sometimes I reach a point when I realize that my prayer does not suit some larger purpose God has in mind that I am not presently capable of understanding and I stop praying for that item. Abraham realized that asking God to spare Sodom for less than ten righteous people was not appropriate in view of the seriousness of their crimes.

PRAYER IS CONNECTING WITH GOD

Prayer is not merely naming items to God, nor is it begging; prayer is connecting (in our consciousness) with the highest and noblest Being of all. As I pray for various agencies, churches, and persons, I try to reach an understanding of what God wants for that agency, person, or church. Sometimes I know immediately, but often I don't. Prayer need not be a conflict. When I don't know, I continue with my prayer list or Scripture. I do not always have many hours to devote to my quiet time, so on those days, I pray what I can with what time I have. But I acknowledge that, throughout the day, God is always present and may present me with an unexpected opportunity to point to Him.

Ask God to teach you the difference between begging (which usually involves a personal whim or desire) and persevering. Often only a few words will suffice for one item. Or you may skip an item. Nevertheless, persevering may be the one right thing to do, as Abraham did until he knew the will of God, and as the Canaanite woman did (see Matthew 15:21-28), and as Jesus encouraged us to do in Matthew 7:9-11, Luke 11:5-13, and Luke 18:1-8.

This latter parable is why Jesus concluded His teaching on prayer by questioning, "When the Son of Man comes, will he find that faith on earth?" (verse 8). Will He find a Canaanite woman, or a persistent widow? Jesus preceded His sorrowful question by asking, "Will not God grant justice to His elect who cry to Him day and night? Will He delay to help them?" (verse 7).

PRAYER IS WORK

Real prayer is real work. Paul asked the Roman church "to *agonize* together with me in your prayers to God on my behalf"

(Romans 15:30, emphasis added). He chose a strong word: *agonize*. Epaphras was "always contending for [the Colossian church] in his prayers, so that [the Colossians] can stand mature and fully assured in everything God wills" (Colossians 4:12). I have many challenging tasks in my life: travel, preparation, teaching, and on and on. But my intercession for the kingdom or for God's will is the most difficult time of my day.

I'm not saying that prayer is unpleasant; it is the most pleasant time of my day, in spite of its struggle. I thoroughly enjoy praising (nobody but God likes to hear me sing!), and as I pray, I am in contact with the highest joy of my life, almighty God. As the years have gone by, I have seen much joy in the struggle, actually bringing me to a point where I rejoice in the will of God as He endorses my effort. Can you imagine the joy when *God* rejoices at the point where my will becomes His! This becomes co-joy with God, and that is breathtaking beyond imagination.

To reach that point, very often I precede a request by telling the Lord that as far as I can discern, I am asking on behalf of His work, His kingdom, His sovereignty, as well as my work for Him. It brings me joy above even sharing with my family. God, after all, is our Father and is preparing us for an eternity of joy in His sovereignty.

God delights in our prayers and is patient with our struggle. He honored the persistent Canaanite woman by calling her faith great. In Hebrews 11, He itemized example after example of saints who persisted through difficult circumstances across the broad spectrum of the Old Testament. Some paid a very dear price for their fellowship with God, but that is what they got: genuine fellowship with their Maker, who had an intention for them when He made them.

OBSTACLES TO CONNECTING WITH GOD

Nothing can break God's side of the steely connection He maintains with us. Sin in our lives does not break God's connection on His side, but it can obscure our *sense* of connection with Him. Both overt sin (lust of the flesh, lust of the eyes, and so forth) and subtle, hidden sin (pride, deceit, and many others) make our sense of connection with God murky. We can restore our awareness of connection by confessing our sin.

Distraction can also block our ability to sense connection with God. Satan knows that we can do much Christian work in the flesh or to be noticed. He does not want us to get God involved through prayer: "Be sober! Be on the alert! Your adversary the Devil is prowling around like a roaring lion, looking for anyone he can devour" (1 Peter 5:8). Satan will work on prayer harder than on almost any Christian endeavor. You probably have experienced diversion from prayer for some "logical" reason. For example, you may become distracted by a current problem, planning your day, or grogginess. An obstacle places us in the darkness that is unawareness of our Maker and Redeemer. John tells us that practicing the truth places us back in the light:

> *This, then, is the judgment: the light has come into the world, and people loved darkness rather than the light because their deeds were evil. For everyone who practices wicked things hates the light and avoids it, so that his deeds may not be exposed. But anyone who lives by the truth comes to the light, so that his works may be shown to be accomplished by God.* (JOHN 3:19-21)

Anyone who has ever experienced being in a lower room of a large cave when all lights are extinguished knows the strange terror of suddenly experiencing total darkness. Almost everywhere we go, some light helps our way. Stepping into sin, distraction, or even sleep plunges us into a semi-darkness, at the least. This book is an invitation to step into the full light of day.

MAINTAINING OUR PART IN PRAYER

Once again, to summarize the four points at the beginning of this chapter:

1. Faith is mediated by the Holy Spirit as a gift.
2. With true faith comes a thrilling sense of reality.
3. Faith is grown through knowledge of Christ.
4. The Word of God is necessary to develop and grow faith.

If you are trying to assimilate these four truths, we can now add a fifth and a sixth:

5. Faith is accomplished when we do our part in connecting with God. His truth is fact; our job is to accept His Word.
6. The climax of all these arrives in Jesus' command to be alert in prayer.

Once again, prayer requires effort. Study closely each of the following Scriptures:

Stay awake and pray, so that you won't enter into temptation. The spirit is willing, but the flesh is weak. (Matthew 26:41)

Be alert at all times, praying that you may have strength to escape all these things that are going to take place and to stand before the Son of Man. (LUKE 21:36)

Devote yourselves to prayer; stay alert in it with thanksgiving. (COLOSSIANS 4:2)

Note how often *alertness* is exhorted. The disciples in the Garden of Gethsemane were not alert; they slept. Jesus' terrible burden in that garden might have been eased if the disciples had remained alert and prayed for Him. Jesus died alone, with the disciples fleeing, yet without help He finished the most difficult work of all time. How easy it is today for our prayers to become routine, both privately and corporately.

God has already done His part. It may take a resolution new to your experience, but God is eagerly waiting to hear from you, on His terms. He will show great patience until you come to His terms. Do your part in connecting with God.

Deborah sang, "May those who love Him be like the rising of the sun in its strength" (Judges 5:31). Jesus affirmed to His disciples, "You are the light of the world. . . . Let your light shine before men, so that they may see your good works and give glory to your Father in heaven" (Matthew 5:14,16). Do your part in connecting with God. In my experience, it takes persistence to develop this sense of reality. It took me considerable time. But if you persevere, the path brightens as you go along.

CHAPTER NINE

THE DESTINY OF FAITH

Search for the LORD and for His strength;
seek His face always.
1 CHRONICLES 16:11

WHAT MATTERS IS HOW THE STORY ENDS

Why such a struggle for faith? Isn't the Christian life easier if we simply accept the seen rather than a so-called struggle to get to the unseen? In this chapter, we shall look at the ultimate outcome of the life of faith. You may want to wait to see those results before you weigh the life of the "seen" as opposed to the "unseen."

God has you in entelechy, a process of sanctification, which will culminate at the end of your life. Entropy means decaying; entelechy involves mounting ever higher and higher. For the present, you can see only the varying circumstances of your life. We work for a completed development that cannot be seen at present but which the Bible hints at strongly when we join Christ in the great highlight — physical death — of our lives. It is easy to place our attention on the varying circumstances instead of on the promise of God for eternity.

LOOK to GOD, NOT CIRCUMSTANCES

To climax all the dimensions of faith we have outlined, we must approach our prayer from God's viewpoint rather than that of our desires. Real faith keeps its eye on God rather than the object(s) being prayed for. I have referred several times to Jehoshaphat's end to his prayer in 2 Chronicles 20:12, "We do not know what to do, but we look to You." Jehoshaphat prayed not for victory but for God's hand, whatever it might be.

I have heard it taught that real faith will produce healing, a promotion, the cure for a broken marriage, and a job and resolve many other crises we face in life. The wonder is that often these ideal requests fall within the will of God and we do see a resolution to the predicament. However, David's son was not healed (see 2 Samuel 12:16-18) and James' and John's request to sit at Jesus' right hand was not answered (see Mark 10:36-40). Sometimes our desires lie so deep in our hearts that our eyes are on self (naturally and unconsciously) rather than on some ultimate purpose that only God knows.

At these times, it is very difficult to trust the wisdom of God rather than the intensity of our own desires. Trust accompanies faith. I have observed this kind of trust in a very few seasoned saints, and whenever I encounter it, I also see a rest — not a resignation to fate but real confidence and dependence on the continuing goodness of God, regardless of circumstances.

FAITH PRODUCES HOLINESS AS OUR WAY OF LIFE

So what does faith produce, and is it desirable? Faith is our introduction to a way of life often discussed but seldom realized. It leads to holiness—not to a "holier than thou" attitude but to genuine godlike holiness. Holiness is usually described as separation from the world, and it is that, but seen from heaven's view, holiness is a splendor not seen through normal human eyes: "Give the Lord the glory due His name; worship the Lord in the splendor of His holiness" (Psalm 29:2).[3]

Both testaments contain the command to holiness on the basis that we are to become like Christ; God is holy:

You must be holy because I am holy. (LEVITICUS 11:45)

Consecrate yourselves and be holy. (LEVITICUS 20:7)

As the One who called you is holy, you also are to be holy in all your conduct; for it is written, Be holy, because I am holy. (1 PETER 1:15-16)

Note that the second command contains two commands: one to consecrate or dedicate ourselves, and one to be holy.

GOD SANCTIFIES, WE DEDICATE

The Holy Spirit sanctifies us, and this results in our growth in holiness. Only God can ultimately *sanctify*, but we can *dedicate*. God takes what we have dedicated or consecrated to Him and moves the process of sanctification forward.

When God made this distinction clear to me, many years ago, I dedicated my body, every part, to Him. It is a delight in prayer to remember 1 Timothy 2:8: "I want the men in every place to pray, lifting up holy hands without anger or argument." Since that time, my wife and I dedicated every house we owned. Interestingly enough, the primary result of our act of dedication was not divine protection but inner contentment in that aura of holiness that accompanies God's continuing work in sanctification.

God calls us to holiness because He Himself is holy. Isaiah in the temple heard the seraphim cry, "Holy, holy, holy is the LORD of Hosts; His glory fills the whole earth" (Isaiah 6:3). The four living creatures in Revelation cried, "Holy, holy, holy, Lord God, the Almighty, who was, who is, and who is coming" (4:8).

SANCTIFICATION IS GROWTH IN HOLINESS

At the beginning of our life in Christ, we are holy in an infantile kind of way, and then we grow in holiness until death. The holiness of God is unique; it is infinite from all creation (see 1 Samuel 2:2). Once perceived, the holiness of God thrills beyond human words (see Exodus 15:11). Jeremiah illustrates one side of God's ineffable holiness; he was broken by God's holiness (see Jeremiah 23:9), so it is not only thrilling, it is also terrifying. David sang that glory in a beautiful psalm: "Honor His holy name; let the hearts of those who seek the LORD rejoice" (1 Chronicles 16:10).

We are slowly, in process, being transformed more and more into the image of Christ. The moment we accept His redemption, we are holy. God has called us with a holy calling "not according to our works, but according to His own purpose and grace" (2 Timothy 1:9). We are to "pursue peace with everyone, and holiness — *without it no one will see the Lord*" (Hebrews

THE DESTINY OF FAITH 93

12:14, emphasis added). Holiness will affect our behavior: "Since [this creation is] to be destroyed in this way, it is clear what sort of people you should be in holy conduct and godliness" (2 Peter 3:11-12).

Clearly, holiness is not a feeling but a fact. That is why faith works so powerfully with holiness. Once we are redeemed, we accept our new holiness by faith. Faith deals only with reality; the Holy Spirit makes real to us both our salvation and our holiness. We cannot be indwelt by the Spirit without being holy.

SIN INTERRUPTS the PROCESS of SANCTIFICATION

At times we sin, which violates our holiness, a grief to the Holy Spirit who is there with us through the process of our offense. If He were at a distance, it would not be a grief to Him; it is a grief because He is present in the process of our transgression. He is leading us constantly, and that is why we are to pray to not be led into sin.

But God's forgiveness is total. He forgets our sin (see Isaiah 43:25; Jeremiah 31:34; Hebrews 10:17). In other words, He annihilates what went before yet leaves us in this tempting environment because He loves overcomers. When we sin, we do not lose our holiness; we remain situated in Christ. Nevertheless, sin interrupts the process of sanctification. The moment we confess our sin, the process is set back in motion. Holiness is at the foundation of God's character and it is truly the foundation of our character.

SANCTIFICATION RESULTS IN NOBILITY

As we progress through our private story, we grow in nobility, which is a subject much neglected in preaching. The children of God are the nobility of the universe. God Himself bestows that nobility on His children. We are members of His royal family.

God is the ultimate and highest nobility, the High King. Isaiah cried,

> *Woe is me, for I am ruined, because I am a man of unclean lips and live among a people of unclean lips, and because my eyes have seen the King, the LORD of Hosts.* (6:5)

God's lofty rank terrified Isaiah. We must recover this sense of reverence.

God has covered the heavens with His majesty (see Psalm 8:1). Asaph sang of His majesty and resplendence (see 76:4). God is the High King above all (see 10:16). Being perfectly holy, He is the King of glory (see 24:10). The people of God will live forever with the Son of God as their Prince (see Ezekiel 37:25). The Lord Jesus is Messiah the Prince (see Daniel 9:25). Jesus is the Source of Life (see Acts 3:15). God has exalted Him to His right hand as ruler and Savior (see 5:31).

HEIRS OF THE HIGH KING

Most astounding of all, God has designated us as His heirs. The Holy Spirit "is the down payment of our inheritance" (Ephesians 1:14), which is an indication of our nobility. We are to give "thanks to the Father, who has enabled [us] to share in the saints' inheritance in the light" (Colossians 1:12). We are to do our work enthusiastically, "knowing that [we] will receive the reward of an inheritance from the Lord" (3:24). Our inheritance comes from the ultimate in nobility, from the Most High God. Athletes exercise self-control to receive a perishable crown (see 1 Corinthians 9:25); we exercise self-control to receive "an inheritance that is imperishable, uncorrupted, and unfading, kept in heaven for you" (1 Peter 1:4).[4] Not only do we have an inheritance but we are co-heirs with Christ.

> *The Spirit Himself testifies together with our spirit that we are God's children, and if children, also heirs — heirs of God and co-heirs with Christ — seeing that we suffer with Him so that we may also be glorified with Him.* (ROMANS 8:16-17)

Paul declares that "the Gentiles are co-heirs, members of the same body, and partners of the promise in Christ Jesus through the gospel" (Ephesians 3:6).

THE ACCOUTREMENTS OF NOBILITY

God has reinforced the idea of our nobility by providing the accoutrements of nobility, including a crown:

> *You will be a glorious* crown *in the LORD's hand, and a royal* diadem *in the palm of your God.* (ISAIAH 62:3, EMPHASIS ADDED)

> *Everyone who competes exercises self-control . . . to receive a perishable* crown, *but we an imperishable one.* (1 CORINTHIANS 9:25, EMPHASIS ADDED)

> *In the future, there is reserved for me the* crown of righteousness, *which the Lord, the righteous Judge, will give me on that day, and not only to me, but to all those who have loved His appearing.* (2 TIMOTHY 4:8, EMPHASIS ADDED)

Blessed is a man who endures trials [perseverance again], because when he passes the test he will receive the crown of life *that He has promised to those who love Him.* (JAMES 1:12, EMPHASIS ADDED)

When the chief Shepherd appears, you will receive the unfading crown of glory. (1 PETER 5:4, EMPHASIS ADDED)

God also gives us the vesture of nobility: "He has clothed me with the garments of salvation and wrapped me in a robe of righteousness" (Isaiah 61:10). Job claimed to be clothed in righteousness: "My just decisions were like a robe and a turban" (Job 29:14). Jesus recognized the righteous in Sardis: "They will walk with Me in white, because they are worthy. In the same way, the victor will be dressed in white clothes" (Revelation 3:4-5). In answer to John's question, the elder informed him, "These are the ones coming out of the great tribulation. They washed their robes and made them white in the blood of the Lamb" (Revelation 7:14).

WE SHALL REIGN WITH CHRIST

If we have all these trappings of royalty, it is small wonder that we shall reign with Christ. Fathom the significance of reigning with Christ! Paul's confidence in this is shown as he was approaching death in a Roman prison. He wrote Timothy, "If we endure, we will also reign with Him" (2 Timothy 2:12). God must have known that many of us would fall, as His Word includes so many admonitions to endurance and perseverance. Jesus promises that "the victor will never be harmed by the second death" (Revelation 2:11). We have to be overcomers now, in this life.

The overcomers will even sit with Jesus on His throne. He declares, "The victor: I will give him the right to sit with Me on My throne, just as I also won the victory and sat down with My Father on His throne" (3:21). So we will not only have robes and crowns, which will be more meaningful to us after we have fully comprehended the spiritual, we will also be co-heirs with Christ. We will in reality sit on Jesus' throne with Him! By God's own word, we are the nobility of the universe, not apparent to the world at present but wonderfully splendid in eternity. Our royal insignia will be visible in a way that we cannot presently imagine.

The psalmist understood and took pleasure in our nobility: "As for the holy people who are in the land, they are the noble ones in whom is all my delight" (Psalm 16:3). James expressed our nobility much later: "If you really carry out the royal law prescribed in Scripture, You shall love your neighbor as yourself, you are doing well" (2:8). As children of the High King, we should consider all the commands of Jesus to be royal law.

The book of Proverbs constantly reveals our nobility:

Listen, for I speak of noble things, and what my lips say is right. (8:6)

It is certainly not good to fine an innocent person,
or to beat a noble for his honesty.
The intelligent person restrains his words,
and one who keeps a cool head
is a man of understanding. (17:26-27)

Isaiah concurs:

A noble person plans noble things; he stands up for noble causes. (32:8)

CHARACTERISTICS OF NOBILITY

From these hints, we can highlight a few characteristics of true Christian nobility. These highlight the life of faith, the life of seeing the unseen:

1. Noble Christians watch their tongue; they think before they speak.
2. Noble Christians are concerned with otherness. They put the good of others before their own.
3. Nobility does not disdain or look down on anyone in an inferior position.
4. Noble Christians make their plans with their environment (church, family, and so forth) in mind.
5. Nobility respects and obeys those in authority.
6. Noble Christians love their brother or sister in Christ. They are active in expressing their love in a perceptible way.
7. Nobility always depends and looks to the highest of all nobility: the High King, our God.
8. Nobility thinks. Noble Christians keep their wits about them, even in crisis.

Just as an earthly monarch always keeps his or her kingdom and the subjects of the kingdom in mind, we who are God's family must regard the concern of our churches or families or whatever organizations we serve as superior to our personal interests.

How often we observe the opposite: people vying for position, struggling only for monetary rewards, seeking notoriety, demanding their own way, and many other vagaries that humans are subject to. An earthly king or queen would carefully avoid behavior that is common — common not merely in the sense of vulgarity but even in the particular misbehaviors common to most all of us. As nobility we can overlook a slight, grant pardon when it is not asked for and elevate true nobility when we perceive it.

MAIN CHARACTERISTICS OF FAITH

Nobility is achieved when we exercise the faith common to the New Testament. A real believer actually, presently, believes all of the following points.

1. Real faith depends not on what is seen but also on many factors that are unseen.
2. The unseen spiritual controls the seen physical.
3. People believe what they *want* to believe. Pray that God will help you want the best, from His standpoint. Down through the ages, the great saints have longed for pure spiritual eyes.
4. We pray that we can "listen" as we read the Bible or hear a sermon.
5. We try to avoid what the "natural" person sees.
6. We accept the blessing of greater "sight" when God moves us into it. We are confident or assured through the Word of God or through any outside source.
7. We pray that the Holy Spirit will impart to us a sense of reality while we are praying.

8. Because the Lord Jesus is the Author and Finisher of our faith, we deliberately study His life and teaching. The Holy Spirit will magnify Jesus. Jesus was humble in spirit. The most ignored of all His teaching is that the least will be the greatest and the first will be last (see Matthew 5:19; 19:30).

9. We do not worry about weak faith; power is perfected in weakness. The leper told Jesus, "Lord, if You are willing, You can make me clean" (Matthew 8:2). When the disciples could not heal the demon-possessed boy, Jesus healed him in the weakness of the father's and the disciples' faith. Faith need be only the size of a mustard seed, as several of Jesus' healings demonstrate.

10. Faith will look to God, not a future expectation.

11. Faith will see God as a great Trinity with His fundamental basis of otherness (as well as oneness).

12. Faith will seek the humility and love that are basic to God's otherness. Jesus was humble in spirit (see Matthew 11:29).

13. Faith will inculcate otherness in all its relationships.

14. Faith will see its own growth in the light of process (entelechy) and so will not be jealous of others' great faith. Entelechy is going on when we recognize that we are maturing in faith.

Biblical faith does not come easily. Endurance is imperative. Jesus' dealing with the Canaanite woman (see Matthew 15:21-28) is illustrative of God's method. Jesus repeatedly tested her to teach the disciples the importance of endurance. He ended the story by announcing to His slow-to-learn disciples that her faith was great.

It takes time and repeated effort to develop a sense of reality that God is present and at work in our lives. Nevertheless, the struggle is worth the effort. To maintain that sense of reality, remind yourself at the beginning of your prayer time and all through it that:

1. God, being omnipresent, is with me, whether I sense His presence or not.
2. It was God who made the magnificent promises in the Bible.
3. God, being infinite Truth, always keeps His promises.
4. I cannot and will not judge God on the basis of His "answers."
5. I will persevere in asking for the sense of reality with God.

We end with new nobility that pleases God. Many great saints of history have left a lasting record of the joy that accompanies strong effort. That delight is not self-generated; it is the same joy that God has when we do His work in prayer. The highest of all joys is co-joy with God. Will you work with Him to hasten His kingdom and establish His sovereignty for all to see?

Only God can bestow that blessing. "Anyone who comes to him must believe that he exists and that he rewards those who earnestly seek him" (Hebrews 11:6, NIV). It may require a long time and much endurance to realize the reality of this verse. Our destiny relies on our fulfilling the meaning of all these biblical passages.

God planned this destiny for us. Our ultimate joy and happiness lies in realizing and demonstrating His glory. He will share it with us in eternity and even now if we fasten our eyes on Him, the Great Unseen. We perceive God now in faith, a faith in His ultimate purposes and glory. The world sees the Great Unseen and the joy of His glory through us.

NOTES

1. See my book *The Mind of Christ: The Transforming Power of Thinking His Thoughts* (Nashville: Broadman, Holman, 1995).
2. See Psalm 40:6-8; 51:16; Isaiah 1:11-17; Hosea 6:6; Micah 6:6-8; Habakkuk 2:4; see also Romans 7:14 — "the law is spiritual."
3. See another reference to the splendor (or beauty) of holiness in 1 Chronicles 16:29-30.
4. Crowns in the Roman world were wreaths woven from perishable plants that faded, such as ivy or laurel.

ABOUT THE AUTHOR

T. W. Hunt is a former prayer specialist with LifeWay Christian Resources and also served on the faculty of Southwestern Baptist Theological Seminary. He is the author of *The Mind of Christ* and a contributor to the *Disciple's Study Bible*. He is coauthor with his daughter, Melana Hunt Monroe, of *From Heaven's View*. Dr. Hunt received his master's and PhD degrees from the University of North Texas. He currently lives with his daughter and her family in Conroe, Texas.

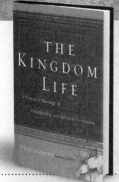

DATE DUE
